Praise for
*A Short Walk to the Edge of Life*

"Think Robert Frost meets *The Worst-Case Scenario* handbook. Reading *A Short Walk to the Edge of Life* took me on the worst possible 'road not taken,' and even though I feel beaten up and drained emotionally, my spirits are lifted. Indeed, his journey has made all the difference."

—ERIC BLEHM, *New York Times* best-selling
author of *Fearless*

"I feel and understand the writer's suffering as he clung to life in a most rugged environment. While Scott Hubbartt expresses disappointments, he still was willing to pursue the ideal point of his destination. As a Holocaust survivor, I can relate his determination to mine. In my own way I, too, walked to the edge of life. When people are in a peril of life, Scott Hubbartt's book *A Short Walk to the Edge of Life* could serve them well in reaching their attainable goals. I strongly endorse this book."

—BORIS KACEL, author of *From Hell to Redemption*

"A true story that makes a compelling read. Scott Hubbartt tells it as it happened. A real-life experience and a refreshing change from the mundane."

—NORMAN BRACKENRIDGE, volunteer in humanitarian
endeavors worldwide

"This is a gripping, real-life account of retired air force veteran Scott Hubbartt, who set off on foot for what he thought would be a simple day hike. Instead, the trek became a near-death experience. Readers will find his telling of the journey—and its unexpected and dramatic detour—is as entertaining as it is profound. You are drawn into the story, feeling as if you are walking with Scott along the treacherous slopes of the Andes or tasting the last drops of life-giving water when his very survival is in doubt. Along with witnessing his courage, you will share in Scott's epiphany about faith and love and will celebrate his rescue and recommitment to the things that matter most in life. This is a must-read story that will entertain and inspire with each turn of the page!"

—LARRY K. GRUNDHAUSER, Brigadier General,
US Air Force (Retired)

"What was meant to be a short walk in the Peruvian puna turned out to be a four-day battle of survival for Scott Hubbartt in which he not only faced the edge of physical endurance in the most difficult conditions but also touched the depths of a man's solitary struggle, both emotionally and spiritually. In this precarious moment, Hubbartt gathered all his strength, hope, and confidence, while turning to higher and divine wisdom. His touching and powerful story is a plea for faith, humility, and gratefulness."

—ERIKA SCHUH, author, traveler,
and international volunteer

SCOTT HUBBARTT

FOREWORD BY COL. TOM BLASE, RETIRED USAF CHAPLAIN

# A SHORT WALK TO THE EDGE OF LIFE

How My Simple Adventure Became a Dance with Death—
and Taught Me What Really Matters

WATERBROOK
PRESS

A SHORT WALK TO THE EDGE OF LIFE
PUBLISHED BY WATERBROOK PRESS
12265 Oracle Boulevard, Suite 200
Colorado Springs, Colorado 80921

All Scripture quotations are taken from the Holy Bible, New International Version®, NIV®. Copyright © 1973, 1978, 1984, 2011 by Biblica Inc.™ Used by permission of Zondervan. All rights reserved worldwide. www.zondervan.com.

Italics in Scripture quotations reflect the author's added emphasis.

Trade Paperback ISBN 978-1-60142-604-8
eBook ISBN 978-1-60142-605-5

Published in the United States by WaterBrook Multnomah, an imprint of the Crown Publishing Group, a division of Random House LLC, New York, a Penguin Random House Company.

WATERBROOK and its deer colophon are registered trademarks of Random House LLC.

Library of Congress Cataloging-in-Publication Data
Hubbartt, Scott.
   A short walk to the edge of life : how my simple adventure became a dance with death —and taught me what really matters / Scott Hubbartt. — First Edition.
       pages cm
   ISBN 978-1-60142-604-8 — ISBN 978-1-60142-605-5 1. Hubbartt, Scott. 2. Christian biography. 3. Mountaineering—Andes. 4. Mountaineering—Peru. 5. Hiking—Andes. 6. Hiking—Peru. I. Title.
   BR1725.H725A3 2014
   248.8'6092—dc23
   [B]

                                                        2013044550

Printed in the United States of America
2014—First Edition

10 9 8 7 6 5 4 3 2 1

SPECIAL SALES
Most WaterBrook Multnomah books are available at special quantity discounts when purchased in bulk by corporations, organizations, and special-interest groups. Custom imprinting or excerpting can also be done to fit special needs. For information, please e-mail SpecialMarkets@WaterBrookMultnomah.com or call 1-800-603-7051.

*For Glenn*

Good people are good because they've come to wisdom through failure. We get very little wisdom from success.

—William Saroyan

He who limps is still walking.

—Stanislaw Jerzy Lec

# Contents

# Foreword

This book captures Scott Hubbartt's story and describes the way almighty God met his needs and answered his prayers through our Lord and Savior Jesus Christ. Scott, a retired air force leader, husband, father, adventurer, and historian, launched a planned ten-mile hike in the Andes mountains and desert of the beautiful country of Peru. Scott's wife, Carolina (Carito), is a native of Peru, and Scott had fallen in love with the homeland of his bride. He planned this supposed eight-hour hike to retrace some of the steps of his wife's ancestors. The walk turned into a struggle for survival and a near-death, five-day ordeal. I know I will never think the same way about a bottle or a drink of water.

In Scott's words, he was trained for, confident about, and even arrogant about this adventurous excursion. But he quickly learned new lessons of humility and faith as he became lost, desperate, and close to death. He simply tried to survive and was prepared to die. He rediscovered that his only help was in the Lord: "I lift up my eyes to the mountains—where does my help come from? My help comes from the LORD, the Maker of heaven and earth" (Psalm 121:1–2).

Scott says that he was saved physically on that journey in the mountains of Peru, but even more important, he was "re-saved" spiritually for a new purpose with renewed Christian passion in his soul.

The apostle Paul wrote to the Philippian church, "For to me, to live is Christ and to die is gain" (Philippians 1:21). Scott was ready to die and sincerely faced his mortality, but then God delivered him. He found new life and was liberated for a renewed purpose as a man of faith.

As you read Scott's story and hear about the background, setting, and events of his five-day excursion, read prayerfully and listen to the message of the miracles of God in Scott's life. But also, on a personal note, ask almighty God to give you a pliable and teachable heart so you can hear and apply the message that God has for you personally.

God bless you.

Tom Blase
Chaplain, Colonel
US Air Force, Retired
March 2013

# And So It Begins

If any of you lacks wisdom, you should ask God, who gives generously to all without finding fault, and it will be given to you. But when you ask, you must believe and not doubt, because the one who doubts is like a wave of the sea, blown and tossed by the wind.

—James 1:5–6

*Wednesday, 2 November 2011, 1950 Hours,*
*Casa Barrera, Trujillo, Perú*
*(8º 06'37.05" S, 79º 01'19.36" W—Elevation 130')*

Journal note that I left at my bedside in the Barrera house the day before my departure:

*2 Nov. 2011, 1950 hours—Trujillo*

*On the eve of my long-awaited adventure to Cerro Pingullo in the western Andes. I am searching for the hamlet of Chepén and Las Minas Casualidad, which are mentioned in my wife's grandfather's [Felipe's] will.*

*As a gringo in Peru, I am an anomaly. A stranger. I have many handicaps—the inability to fluently speak the language not the least of them. Still, I go. There are more intrepid souls, but I figure myself about middle of the road. Still, I go into the unknown in the lower Altiplano of the middle-western Andes.*

*My destination tomorrow is Salpo. From there I hope to explore Carabamba and the hamlet of Chepén. In a day or two I will attempt the descent to Poroto.*

*Felipe did it, who knows how many times. I want to tell my grandchildren about his exploits from firsthand experience.*

*They say I'm crazy. That's OK. I'm just curious and determined.*

*Hubbartt*

- - - - -

I'm just a regular guy. I balance bills, pay a mortgage, and try to be the best father I can be to my three grown daughters as well as an acceptable husband to the perfect wife. But in a nutshell, during a week of November 2011, I messed up big time.

This is my story.

It all started when I went for a walk in the Peruvian puna, which some call the Altiplano and others the Alto Pampa. It's the high desert region of the Andes mountains characterized by dry, barren, windswept, and rocky terrain—where only the hardiest of living things can exist. It was supposed to be an eight- to ten-mile hike along what I expected would be an established, easy-to-follow trail. Instead, I became hopelessly lost and almost died.

After my fifteen visits to Peru, many people regarded me as a kind of expert on travel in that country. I was often complimented on my tales about my adventures in this wonderful land, which is twice the size of Texas. But that's the danger of flattery: over time you start to believe it.

It has been many months since my little expedition, and I am still trying to fully appreciate the gift I was given—*more than life itself,* which we too often take for granted. I now know that God has at least two plans for my life: One is that I was supposed to survive in that desert. Second, I am to share my story with anyone who will listen.

# Searching for a Lost Gold Mine

"Because he loves me," says the LORD, "I will rescue him;
I will protect him, for he acknowledges my name.
He will call on me, and I will answer him;
I will be with him in trouble,
I will deliver him and honor him.
With long life I will satisfy him
and show him my salvation."

—Psalm 91:14–16

*Monday, 31 October 2011, 2230 Hours,*
*Aeropuerto Jorge Chávez, Lima, Perú*
*(12° 01'23.15" S, 77° 06'30.16" W—Elevation 95')*

I love adventure and travel, which are probably the main reasons I ended up fighting for my life in the Peruvian Andes.

As long as I can remember, I've never been able to stay put in one place for very long. So maybe it's in my genes, because I come from a long line of immigrants and travelers who were always on the move.

When I was a child, our family of six often packed up the Dodge and set off on cross-country road trips. I *absolutely loved* these journeys. One of our best trips was a drive from California to Iowa, where my dad grew up, and then on to New England to visit my mom's family, followed by a sweep through the South on our way home.

My two older brothers had dibs on the window seats in the back, with our little sister between them. So my usual place was in the middle of the front seat with a road map on my lap. I relished the great view, and whenever we crossed a state line, I would stretch my legs as far forward as possible to ensure that I was there first.

My desire for adventure and love for the outdoors drew me to the Boy Scouts. Then after high school I enlisted in the US Air Force, partly so that I might see more of the world as part of my job.

In those days I never imagined I would visit Peru, but early in 1981 while stationed in South Dakota, I caught a glimpse of a beautiful girl, a fellow airman who took my breath away. I later learned that her name was Carolina and that in the 1970s she had immigrated to the United States from Peru. Things worked out well between us, and a year later my "Carito" became *mi vida*—my wife.

This was the beginning of my love affair with Peru.

From our first days together, Carito often shared with me stories of her homeland, and I grew increasingly enchanted with this exotic place. We first visited Peru together in 1986, traveling with our first daughter, Christina, then just an infant. We were able to see Lima as well as the city of Trujillo in the north.

I immediately fell in love with the vast, diverse, and alluring country. I also was intrigued by the stories of Carito's family, especially her entrepreneurial grandfather, Felipe Lám, who himself was an immigrant from China, coming to Peru in 1908.

Sadly, I was not able to visit Peru again for any extended period in the next eighteen years.

- - - - -

In December 2004, shortly after I retired from the air force, I finally returned to Peru for an extended visit. Accompanied by several of Carito's sisters and a brother, we traveled overland, crisscrossing the country from Lima to Arequipa and on to Puno, which hugs the edge of Lake Titicaca. We then ventured to Cuzco, where I visited the majestic and mystical Incan city of Machu Picchu. From there it was back to Lima and on to

Trujillo. My fascination with the country was sealed, and after that I returned at least once or twice a year.

Over time I traversed the country from top to bottom, across its three regions—up and down the coast, over the Andes, and into the Amazon regions. I absorbed as much of its culture, history, mouth-watering cuisine, and geography as possible. I simply could not get enough!

## Planning the Short Walk

After yet another satisfying two-week visit together to her homeland in the fall of 2011, Carito and I had to part. She had to return to the States for a tour of duty, and I had to decide what adventure to pursue with my two remaining weeks in my beloved Peru. Still actively serving in the air force reserve, Carito needed to finish her final tour, and we looked forward to her completion of a wonderful twenty-two-year military career.

We had been visiting Cajamarca and then staying in Trujillo, in northern Peru, so we took a 350-mile bus trip south along the coast to Lima so Carito could catch her flight home.

In Lima, while we waited at the airport, Carito asked, "What are you going to do with your remaining time in Peru?"

Off the cuff I replied, "Maybe I'll retrace your grandfather Felipe's walk from Poroto to Salpo." Then, to make my boast sound more plausible, I added, "But I'm thinking of doing it the easy way... I might do it in reverse and walk from the Sierra into the valley—all downhill."

"Honey, just be careful, and *please* use a guide," she replied.

Sometimes I'm a poor listener. This was one of those times.

I walked with Carito to the airport security station to see her off for the seven-hour overnight flight to Texas. Had either of us known it might be our last parting, it would have been different. Instead, we casually hugged, shared a quick kiss, and promised to see each other again in a few weeks.

– – – – –

A few hours later I was on a bus for the eleven-hour return trip to Trujillo, all the while pondering what to do with the next couple of weeks. I dwelt on our conversation in the airport and my dream to trace her grand-father's steps one day…and then suddenly I knew it was what I wanted to do! As an amateur historian and genealogist with a curious nature, I hoped to learn more about my wife's culture and family history.

For years I had listened intently when *mi suegra*—my mother-in-law, Evelina—talked about growing up in Peru and her Chinese immigrant father, Felipe Lám. A gentle, wise, and wholly good woman, Evelina always spoke of her father with kindness and a daughter's love. She helped me fill in so many gaps in the family historical narrative. Especially intriguing to me were her stories of Felipe's many talents and successes, including the businesses and properties he owned. And then there was that mystery concerning his rumored gold mines.

Trained in traditional Chinese medicine and fluent in several languages, Felipe was an opportunist. He never limited himself simply to opening a small stall in the town market to peddle herbal remedies. Instead, he sought out and seized opportunities wherever he found them, which served him well in his new country.

Born in 1890, Felipe grew up in the southern Chinese region of Guangdong, not far from present-day Hong Kong and Macao. Felipe stood apart from many Chinese immigrants in that he was well educated and ambitious.

Felipe eventually settled in the small town of Chepén, in northern Peru, on the well-traveled crossroad between Trujillo, Chiclayo, and Cajamarca. There his ambition, talents, and natural skills quickly established him in the community. Felipe realized this opportunity was a precious gift and if he applied himself, it would bring prosperity. And in time Felipe did prosper. He started several businesses, secured properties, and eventually married a local girl, Catalina Hernandez-Vasquez. Before long

Felipe Lám, the Chinese immigrant to Peru who
owned a gold mine named Las Minas Casualidad.

they were blessed with three children: a son, Próspero (meaning "prosperity"), and two daughters, Mery and Evelina.

Initially Felipe was content with life in Chepén and worked well with both the Chinese and Peruvian communities as well as the surrounding Jequetepeque Valley farmers. He owned a fine home, which had an attached corner store, in Chepén at 13 Guadalupe Street. In the back garden of his home stood the largest mango tree in the neighborhood, which Evelina often recalled whenever she shared her childhood memories.

In the early 1920s, when Próspero was old enough for the trip, the boy was sent with an uncle to China. He lived there with relatives and was educated in the traditional language and customs. Sadly, a few years later word came that eighteen-year-old Próspero had died of heart trouble. While the details were murky, Evelina believed that he died of loneliness and a broken heart. Tragedy and sadness were not new to Felipe, and they would soon visit him again.

Around 1930, Felipe's wife, Catalina, died at the age of thirty-five. This left him with two young daughters to care for. On the heels of this loss, the ripples of the global depression reached Peru. Every businessman and industry felt the strain, and Felipe was no exception.

Before long Felipe married a woman named Celina, and then he inexplicably moved his small family more than ninety miles south to Poroto, a small town east of Trujillo in the Andean foothills. Poroto is set in a fertile mountain valley where it hugs the Río Moche and is joined by an almost always dry river called Río Chepén. Poroto is known for little more than sugarcane and pineapples, but the village also serves as a stopping place along the winding road from Trujillo to the high mining towns of Salpo, Otuzco, and Cajabamba—all hardscrabble settlements filled with rough men seeking fortunes in the canyons and rocky mines scattered across nearby hillsides.

The exact reasons for Felipe's move to Poroto are unclear. While there were few (if any) Chinese in the community, Felipe seems to have prospered there and again established a home and even a store on the town square as well as other properties.

This was about all I could find out about Felipe—until his will surfaced.

## Sorting Facts from Legends

On one of my earlier trips to Peru, I had spent some time in Chepén trying to dig up details of Felipe's life. For so long the many Chinese immigrants in Peru, much like other immigrants around the world, were treated like second-class citizens. Consequently, few written records have survived.

Luckily, Felipe Lám came to Peru, not as an indentured servant, but as an educated man and went on to become a successful businessman, property owner, and merchant. In Chepén I uncovered the birth certificates of his three children and located the home the Lám family had lived in during the 1920s and 1930s.

Evelina was a young girl in 1937 when Felipe died of stomach cancer at the age of fifty-six. Most mysterious of her memories of her father was that among the properties he owned was at least one mine in the western Sierra. The mountain town of Salpo was often mentioned in the sketchy and fluid retelling of stories about the mysterious mine.

Owning a mine in Peru carries with it the possibility of untold riches. The Peruvian Sierra is filled with many commercial minerals, not the least of which are gold and silver. Over the decades political upheaval and chaos have often been the norm in Peru. Evelina understood that the property, having never been formally or legally registered and then being abandoned, likely had been sold off by the government long ago. As a result she would have no existing claim to it.

Still, the mysterious story of this mine intrigued us all.

— — — — —

One day I was going through one of the many boxes of unsorted notes and files on our family histories when I came across an unexpected treasure: Felipe Lám's will.

I found it among Evelina's papers, along with Carito's tattered birth certificate and other miscellaneous papers. Looking over the thick document that comprised his will, and despite the fact that my Spanish has never been good, I immediately recognized it for what it was: *El Último Testamento de Felipe Lám* (the Last Testament of Felipe Lám).

Excited, I quickly plowed through the document. I not only learned the names of Felipe's parents but also discovered that he specifically mentioned among his assets a mine named Las Minas Casualidad, meaning the "chance" or "hazard" mines, and included clues to its location.

In his will Felipe stated that Las Minas Casualidad was near Cerro Pingullo, also known as El Cauro. Finally I had something tangible to work with! So I immediately began searching for more details about the mine. While I had no illusions of making a claim on the mine in the name of the family, I thought that gathering more details about its history would be a wonderful addition to the family narrative. Wherever Las Minas Casualidad was, I longed to learn more about it—and perhaps someday to locate it.

## Preparing to Depart

After the long bus ride from Lima, I returned to Trujillo to the home of my sister-in-law Sheila and her husband, José.

My plan was simple. I would take a bus to the mining town of Salpo and from there make my way to the high puna (plateau) hamlet of Chepén de Salpo. From Chepén, I would descend on foot to the village of Poroto. I would be hiking along the eleven-thousand-foot-high puna of the coastal Andes and then descending into and through the deep canyons leading to the Río Chepén valley. I would end my trek at Poroto—nine thousand feet lower than the Chepén in the puna.

I estimated it would be a ten-mile stroll, eight hours at the most, and all downhill. I felt supremely confident and qualified. It would be a day-long walk—a walk in the park. What could go wrong?

I foresaw no problems. A piece of cake. Simple.

The evening before my departure, as was the custom when I stayed with José and Sheila, we ate dinner together. Their cook, Flor, usually prepared a mouth-watering meal. However, to my disappointment, this night she served me liver. I really don't like liver—not at all! And to make matters worse, this was not just a small piece of meat smothered in onions. It was a huge serving that lapped over my dinner plate on all sides.

*With so many terrific Peruvian dishes available,* I thought, *why liver?* But I love Flor's cooking, so I ate my half pound of liver with a smile. I had no idea that this liver feast would be my last solid meal for many days.

Sitting there at the family table after our meal, I told José and Sheila of my plans to head into the mountains the next morning. They weren't excited about my journey. If it had been anyone else, I think they would have made more of a fuss, but they had come to expect some impulsive, even crazy ideas from me. I assured them I would be careful and should be back in two or three days.

Afterward I went upstairs to pack my knapsack. I started with a topographical map and two compasses—it's always good to have a backup. I made sure I had a couple of knives, a large camping towel, some underwear and socks, a heavy paperback book—*The Winds of War* by Herman Wouk—a National Geographic world map, a yellow poncho, a Tilley hat, two Ziploc bags, and a plastic solar blanket. I usually carry one of these dollar-shop-quality solar blankets when I travel, although I had yet to use one and wasn't even sure how or if it would work. I also packed a small bottle of ancient military-surplus water-purification tablets encased in cracking wax, some matches, a length of nylon cord, and a razor blade. Last I threw in my iPod and camera.

I consider myself a seasoned traveler and am accustomed to austere conditions. I have suffered from typhoid, trichinosis, ticks, food poisoning, dengue (breakbone), and Guáitira fever, as well as arbitrary arrest and extortion by corrupt police officials. Looking at my gear, I felt I was overprepared, but I thought, *In Peru you can never be too careful.*

It was early spring in the Peruvian Andes, so I figured the weather shouldn't be an issue. I believed I'd come across people and settlements on my trekking route, which meant access to food, water, and shelter if I needed them.

*Yeah, I'm up for this. Ten miles, five to eight hours, all downhill. A walk in the park.*

# Day I

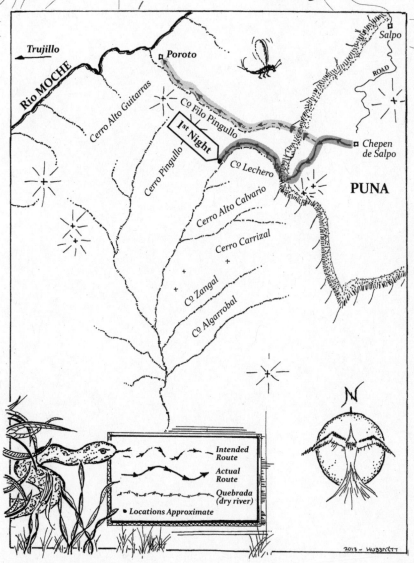

Trujillo

Rio MOCHE

Poroto

Salpo

ROAD

Cerro Alto Guitarras

Cº Filo Pingullo

1st Night

Chepen de Salpo

Cerro Pingullo

Cº Lechero

PUNA

Cerro Alto Calvario

Cerro Carrizal

Cº Zangal

Cº Algarrobal

Intended Route

Actual Route

Quebrada (dry river)

• Locations Approximate

N

2013 - HUBBNETT

# 3

# I'm Off!

Don't let schooling interfere with your education.

—Mark Twain

*Thursday, 3 November 2011, 0415 Hours,*
*Casa Barrera, Trujillo, Perú*
*(8° 06'37.05" S, 79° 01'19.36" W—Elevation 130')*

I awoke at 4:15 a.m. before my alarm had gone off. I've always been an early riser and often wake up without an alarm clock. I relish the morning quiet. It's a special time for me, *my* time, a time to organize my thoughts and contemplate the day ahead. Today, however, I had a bus to catch.

I quickly dressed, grabbed my knapsack, and rushed downstairs, careful not to wake my hosts. On the way out I grabbed a two-and-a-half-liter bottle of water from the table but walked past my coat, which was hanging on a nearby chair. I emerged into quiet, predawn Trujillo, gently swinging the steel gate shut and locking it behind me. I dutifully tossed the keys up the inside steps, and as I did so, I remembered my coat on the chair upstairs. I considered waking José but decided against it, reasoning that the early morning chill would soon burn off. After all, if I needed to, I could always buy a wool poncho or a sweater along the way—or so I reasoned.

I had no trouble hailing a cab and arrived at the combi-bus station in just a few minutes, plenty early for the 5:30 a.m. bus to Salpo. The combi—a sort of minibus—would take me east from Trujillo, up the Río

Moche valley and into the mountains, and drop me at Salpo, a mining town in the low Andes. From there I planned to gather additional information and details on Chepén, the local conditions, and anything I could learn about the trail to Poroto.

I had long wanted to visit Salpo. The town's name often came up in my genealogy research. Not only did Felipe Lám settle at Poroto, situated along the road up to Salpo, but Felix, my dear father-in-law, was born and grew up in nearby Otuzco, another hill town.

I was also eager to put to rest, at least in my imagination, what had happened to Felipe's gold mine.

## On the Combi

In the Trujillo open-air bus station, I waited with twenty or thirty other passengers—mostly men—all working-class people of the Sierra. I noted that many seemed to be returning to their mountain homes loaded with bundles and boxes stuffed with cherished supplies and foodstuffs.

Shivering from the morning chill, I felt conspicuous. I was the only nonlocal at the bus station and realized I could not hope to blend in. I was clad in thin pants, a light, yellow short-sleeved shirt, and tennis shoes. I was "Mister Adventure" and must have looked ridiculous to these serious, hardy folks. Still, at the time I had other things on my mind. The excitement of my imminent departure and looming adventure had cast its spell on me.

Around 5:30 a.m. a geriatric Dodge minibus pulled up. While we waited to board, the roof of the ancient vehicle was noisily loaded with an array of materials: tools, cases of soda, dry goods, and other bulky cargo. The bus reminded me of an overloaded donkey as it sat there noisily idling. As more and more was stacked on it, the van's suspension groaned and complained like a reluctant beast of burden.

I took a seat near the front, next to a whiskered old man who smiled grandly at me, displaying just three teeth, all alarmingly decayed. He smelled like the dirty-towel bin back in high school gym class. *Wonderful,* I thought.

But as I settled into my hard seat, I was supremely content knowing that *finally* I was on my way. By my reckoning I believed I'd be back in Trujillo in two or three days max. It seemed like a solid plan—*dummy-proof.*

We headed east, and as we left the edges of the sleeping city, the sweet scents of crops, cane, and moist, fertile land worked their way through the cracked and bent window frames of the crowded bus. The faint glow of dawn peeked above the high mountains to our east as we sped through the flat farming region of the Río Moche valley. Lush emerald-green farms of all sizes—sleepy *granjas, chacras,* and *haciendas*—lined both sides of the highway. For eons this has been a prosperous farming valley, and the people here have thrived, due in large part to the Río Moche flowing down from the Andean snowmelt.

I relished moments like these: the sights and smells of the land, the opportunity to wantonly chase my dreams. My expectations for adventure rose like the morning sun. I realized how blessed I was and silently whispered a quick prayer of thanks.

## Looking for Felipe's Las Minas Casualidad

During an earlier visit that year to Peru, I had searched in Lima for more clues to the Las Minas Casualidad by inquiring at the Instituto Geográfico Nacional (National Geographic Institute). Even with access to the most detailed maps of Peru, I could not locate any place known by this name, nor could I find a mountain named Cerro Pingullo. Dispirited, before leaving I had purchased a couple of detailed topographical maps of the northern region encompassing both Chepén and Poroto, towns I knew that Felipe had lived in.

Then I went to the San Borja district of the capital to visit the Ministerio de Energía y Minas (Ministry of Energy and Mines). There I met a pleasant intern named Carlos, who steered me to a massive leather-bound book, probably a foot thick, packed with ancient documents. Carlos explained these were claims for mines during the period I was interested in. "We are modern now, but this stuff is old," he told me apologetically. Each claim was filed as it was received and in no particular order.

A quick glance told me the task was overwhelming. There were hundreds of claims, all handwritten on cracking, disintegrating, yellowed paper. Many had portions missing or were simply unreadable due to damage from age and water. Some were written on the backs of old letters, receipts, and other documents. I knew I would never get through them all.

I asked Carlos if there might be a computer database of these claims.

"No," he said, explaining there was never enough money for such technology. "Besides," he added, "no one cares about such things anymore."

Well, not exactly. There I was—*one.* Searching was worth a try.

After a couple of hours of blurry-eyed and fruitless looking, I returned to Carlos's desk with the massive book. I found an older man perched at this post—Carlos was gone. This polite and professional bureaucrat confided in me that indeed there was a computer database of the names of all mines ever claimed and registered with the ministry.

The man offered me his computer terminal and assisted with my search, and after a few minutes we learned that no formal claim existed for a mine named Casualidad anywhere near the area—or in all of Peru, for that matter.

By that point it was getting late in the day, and I left discouraged.

Later that night, as I sat in a poorly lit café in Lima enjoying a delicious bowl of oxtail soup, accompanied by a cold drink, things finally started to come together. I was looking over my notes, and tucked among them was one of the maps I had bought at the National Geographic Institute. As I finished my dinner, I put the notes away and wondered what

I was missing. I contemplated giving up but then remembered a story—now a Hubbartt family legend—of a time many years back when my father had found a spot in Indiana by systematically looking for a place called Mount Tabor, where some of our ancestors were supposedly buried.

Reflecting on this, I pulled out the topographic map of the area around Poroto, and using the straight edge of a menu, started methodically searching every miniscule annotation on the chart. It was tedious and a bit difficult in the café's dim light, but then, unexpectedly, I came across a small reference that stopped me cold. In the steep mountains rising up to the edge of the puna and southeast of Poroto, I saw clearly marked "C Pingullo." Then almost immediately I saw a small cluster of dwellings labeled "Chepén."

"Wow, *another* Chepén," I whispered to myself.

The village where Felipe initially had lived was almost a hundred miles to the north and also called Chepén. Now, I had found another Chepén. What a coincidence! I sat back and tried to absorb all this.

Chepén is an unusual name. It comes from the ancient Moche language, and I wondered what were the chances of an ancient coastal civilization giving the same name to two places, one near the coast and the other on the high plateau of the puna.

Even more exciting was that next to this second Chepén was a small 11,444-foot mountain called Cerro Pingullo—just like the one mentioned in Felipe's will.

Bingo!

## The Two Chepéns

Excited by the discoveries, I continued meticulously examining the map, searching all around the mountain for an annotation of a mine called Casualidad. No luck. It occurred to me that if the mine had never been officially claimed or registered with the government, it was plausible there would be no annotation of Casualidad on official maps. But that didn't mean it didn't exist.

I spent the rest of the evening in that small café carefully scanning my map for clues to this expanding mystery. The existence of a small hamlet, the second Chepén, near Cerro Pingullo, nagged at me. *Why were two places in northern Peru named Chepén?*

Before I could sort it out, the café closed, and I was forced to retreat to my stuffy hotel room next door. The following day the mystery continued to haunt me. I returned to the café of the night before and once again spread out my map on the table. "Okay, okay, break it down," I mumbled to myself.

I recalled that after the news of his son's death, followed by the death of his wife, Felipe had moved from Chepén in the north to Poroto to start a new life. At least one cousin, Juan—who had accompanied Felipe from China twenty years earlier, also moved his family to Poroto. But was there really a future for a businessman and merchant in such a tiny isolated mountain town compared to the bustling coastal town of Chepén?

That led me to my theory, although still not proved, of the two Chepéns.

As I've explained, the first, larger, and better-known Chepén is on the sprawling, fertile, green coastal plains of the Jequetepeque Valley along the busy highway crossroads leading to the cities of Trujillo, Chiclayo, and Cajamarca. This Chepén, with a large Chinese population, was rooted in the regional agriculture and commerce along what came to be known later as the Pan-American Highway.

I later learned that the official name of the *other* Chepén—the Chepén of the high puna, a Chepén I never imagined existed—was Chepén de Salpo. This tiny hamlet, clearly marked on my topographical map, sits high on the windswept plateau above the Río Moche valley. Not far from the settlement is the mountain known as Cerro Pingullo, perched on the very edge of the high puna's precarious drop-off to the valleys far below.

I wondered, *What could possibly be the connection between these two Chepéns—if any?*

## On the Road to Salpo

With the morning now well lit, the old van groaned as we climbed higher into the low Andes. The landscape evolved from the lush green coastal valley to a dusty, khaki-colored panorama of canyon walls and towering mountains that were occasionally broken by deep river valleys lined with small farms.

Mr. Whiskers shuffled his weight to get more comfortable and then leaned his sleepy head on my shoulder. I settled into my seat, careful not to wake my snoring seatmate. It wasn't long before I, too, was dozing pleasantly as the groaning, overloaded Dodge bounced and swayed, winding its way up the two-lane road into the Sierra.

After about two hours a horrible screeching hiss, followed by several alarming knocks and bangs, rudely woke me. The combi lurched to the left and ground to a sudden halt. There was a riot of voices and expletives from passengers jarred awake by the sudden stop. A baby wailed, a dog barked, a man coughed and hacked, and the driver cursed. I thought we had hit something. Mr. Whiskers lifted his head and karate-chopped the web of drool swaying between his chin and my shoulder. He asked me if we had arrived.

Looking out the waxy windows, I noted how dramatically the scenery had changed. We were stopped in a dusty hamlet shrouded in mist and fog. The green of the valley behind us had been replaced with the dingy, dusty browns and grays of a foothill village. The rough adobe structures looked abandoned, but then an ancient man emerged from the shadows, shrouded in a poncho and leading a goat. He loped past us, shaking his head at our dilemma.

Several male passengers excitedly engaged the driver in a conversation.

I thought it best to sit still and see what happened next. That didn't take long. About half the men disembarked and walked to the driver's side of the bus, converging around the left front wheel. A couple of them came back on board and rummaged through a bundle of greasy blankets behind the driver's seat, eventually removing a jack and several heavy tools.

Feeling the need to answer nature's call, I disembarked and relieved myself behind a low wall. Back at the bus I saw the men still clustered tightly around the suspect wheel, all talking at once, with plentiful arm gestures and finger pointing. Peering through the small crowd, I noted, with no small amount of concern, that the vehicle's front wheels were pointed in different directions. It didn't look good.

I watched as the men propped a tiny jack on two small bricks. Within moments the impossibly heavy bus, creaking and groaning, was slowly lifted off the dirt road. Two men scurried underneath and began pounding on something with heavy tools. Certain that disaster was imminent, I stood there and tried to look as if I understood what was going on, nodding whenever it seemed appropriate amid the excited chatter.

When the mountain cold—hovering not far above freezing—became too much, I carefully boarded the bus, thinking I needed to step lightly or I might cause the vehicle to collapse onto the men underneath.

I reached for my pack, which was stuffed in a rack above a girl who looked to be about fourteen. She was nursing a baby. Collecting my bag, I noticed it was wet and saw that the cap to my water bottle was cracked and slowly leaking. I had lost about a fourth of my water. I made a mental note to buy another bottle when I got to Salpo.

After a while the wheel was jockeyed into place. Some wire and pins were passed to the men below, and after about forty-five minutes of jacking, hammering, chattering, pointing, and no small amount of cursing, the men emerged from beneath the old Dodge. The behemoth was suddenly, violently, and unceremoniously dropped, loudly and protesting, onto its tired and ancient struts and bald tires. The passengers hurried

The outskirts of Salpo, where the hills are covered with mines yielding every metal of value.

back aboard, the noisy motor was cranked up—spewing a cloud of blue smoke—and we were again on our way.

Mr. Whiskers smiled and wasted no time reclaiming the resting place for his head on my shoulder.

The old Dodge rattled along, and after thirty bumpy minutes, we neared Salpo. As we rumbled into the outskirts, I noticed a high level of activity on the hillsides on both sides of the road—unexpected, especially at this hour. Large sections of the hills were being crudely scraped and excavated. Along a road creeping up the hills surrounding the village were huge tarps and plastic sheets clumsily strung over crude work sites. The effect reminded me of mildew creeping up the walls of a neglected shower stall in a cheap hotel. Men, pushing impossibly overloaded wheelbarrows, emerged from these sheets and navigated loads of rock and soil to waiting wooden sluices. None of this action appeared organized or symmetrical. This was rough mining in full gear.

The combi came to a stop about a block from the Plaza de Armas—the main town square—and the passengers lazily disembarked. Mr. Whiskers again lifted his head, mumbled something, and gave me a doleful smile before he shuffled off.

I had arrived.

# 4

# The Puna

A lot of people are afraid of heights. Not me, I'm afraid
of widths.

—Steven Wright

*Thursday, 3 November 2011, 0915 Hours,*
*Combi Stop, Salpo, Perú*
*(8° 00'14.03" S, 78° 36'13.21" W—Elevation 11,360')*

Situated on the eastern edge of the high plateau called the puna, Salpo
was pretty much what I had expected: small, rural, and isolated. What
drew anyone here was that the town sat atop a land rich with gold, silver,
tin, iron, and lead. Every metal with commercial worth was being sucked
out of the surrounding hills, mostly by small groups of unionized miners
but independent and illegal ones as well. Mining is big in Peru.

I noted a few men on the street, shovels and sticks in hand, milling
about and drinking from a shared milky-green bottle. *Miners taking a
break,* I thought. Then, at the other end of the street, four men—also
with shovels and a pick—appeared and headed toward me. Since they
were loud, unkempt, and possibly looking for trouble, I did the wisest
thing I could: I quickly sidestepped into a convenient *tiendita,* a small
cubbyhole that served as a family store. The shopkeeper told me it was a
bad time. "There might be trouble—troublemakers," I heard him say
more than once.

I asked for a cup of coffee and was told there was none, so I settled for
a warm soda and took a seat at a rickety wooden table while I considered

my next move. I hoped to use Salpo as a base for a day or so while I inquired about getting to Chepén, farther up on the rugged puna, and perhaps learn about the trail conditions down to Poroto. I asked about a hotel or possibly a room to rent for the night and was told there were none in town. This surprised me. In Trujillo I'd been led to believe there would be no problem getting a room here.

Once the seedy men had disappeared and my soda bottle was empty, I cautiously headed for the town's square a block or so away. If there was a hotel in town, I'd find it there.

The small sloping plaza was drab, dirty, and sad. Other than a couple of youths with motorcycles, a woman selling potatoes, and a few mangy dogs, it didn't offer much. I walked to the *municipalidad,* where a faded sign directed me to the mayor's office. The mayor's young receptionist made it clear that I would not find a place to stay in Salpo. She then turned away and pretended to sort through the random papers in her desk, obviously hoping I'd leave. I tried to engage her and inquired about any villages farther up on the puna, but the woman simply shook her head and repeated, "No, no...*nada.*"

Feeling disappointed and uneasy with the tense atmosphere, I pondered what to do next. While not fully understanding the source of tension in the town, I had spent enough time in South America to know that my best course of action was to follow my instincts and leave as soon as possible.

It was still early, and the only bus returning to Trujillo would not leave for another hour or so. I briefly weighed the option of going back to Trujillo. But I couldn't imagine returning so soon after getting only this far. I hadn't yet encountered any real problems, and there were still so many unanswered questions about Felipe and his mine.

I asked some boys outside the mayor's office about going to Carabamba, the next closest town of any size. They told me I would have to return to Trujillo and take another bus from there to Carabamba, an option that made no sense to me.

Because of the tense atmosphere around the square and the numerous subliminal messages telling me I wasn't welcome, I decided to walk to the cemetery I had noticed on a small hill north of the plaza. Ever the curious genealogist, I remembered that my father-in-law had a sister—or perhaps an aunt—who was buried in or near Salpo. I decided to look at the gravestones and markers there.

The day was getting warmer, and the uphill hike helped throw off the mountain chill penetrating my light clothes. I found the desolate cemetery barren and disorganized, with no apparent plan or order as to how or where its residents were laid to rest. An array of ornate and primitive graves littered the hillside. The scores of markers—interspersed with

The graveyard at Salpo, where I saw firsthand the destruction of ladrónes de nichos (graverobbers).

cactus, thistle, and rubbish—ranged from massive brick, stone, and cement monuments to simple wooden and stick crosses.

I spent about half an hour wandering and weaving between the stones and rubble but found no familiar names. I did, however, notice several graves broken open to reveal aging skeletons and a few newer corpses pulled out into the open. Disgusted, I realized this was the work of the notorious *ladrónes de nichos* (graverobbers). These despicable vermin break into tombs and dig up graves to rob the corpses of whatever jewelry or mementos were buried with them.

As I made my way back to the road leading into town, I came across a large crypt. Topped with a stone cross, the grave seemed intact. However, in an exterior cubicle a human skull sat gaping at me—*creepy*. I impulsively snapped a photo and then quickly left the sad place and headed back to the town square.

## Moto to Chepén

Back at the town plaza, I approached some teens with motorcycles and inquired about going farther up into the puna.

"*¿La puna?*" One of the young men responded, eyebrows raised.

"*Sí. Es posible,*" another one said.

They told me they knew the region well. I then asked about the small hamlet of Chepén, and to my surprise the youths were familiar with the place and told me it would be no problem to take me there. They said the trip would take about an hour.

"*Sí. Me gustaría ir al pueblito de Chepén*" ("Yes. I would like to go to Chepén"), I said.

"*Sí, señor, yo conozco Chepén, pero nadie va por allí.*" ("Yes, sir, I know Chepén, but nobody goes there.")

It would have been good to reflect for a moment on that comment— "nobody goes there"—but I was a man on a mission.

I chose the most reliable looking of the four bikes owned by a guy named Juan, and I secured a ride for a negotiated fee of three sols (about one US dollar). As we prepared to depart, Juan busied himself by strapping my knapsack to the bike's small rear rack. Before I could get securely settled on the small shared seat, Juan said decisively, *"¡Vámonos!"* Then he kicked the bike to life and set off with me hanging tightly to his waist with one arm and my tethered bag with the other.

Within moments we were out of Salpo and negotiating our way along an increasingly bad road. The rough road, really a rocky double track, forced us to travel slowly as we bounced along. We then began to climb, winding and weaving, farther into the high puna. The landscape soon evolved into a moonscape-like appearance. It was barren, treeless, and remote. I felt as though I were on another planet.

The dry tableland, covered with low rocky hills, is indeed bleak and windswept. It is characterized by rock-strewn grasslands and sloping plains, often framed by distant towering snowcapped peaks. The nameless character played by Clint Eastwood in *High Plains Drifter* would fit right in to this setting.

Few creatures and fewer humans live on the puna. The ancient, hardy, isolated natives who live there call themselves *puñeros* (people of the puna) and know little else but that place.

Most of the puna sprawls across a massive elevated plain that covers the southeastern portion of Peru, between the southern city of Arequipa and Puno on the shore of lofty Lake Titicaca. The puna narrows and extends through the high Andes between the coast and the Amazon basin, stretching up to Cajamarca in the north.

East of Trujillo, on Peru's north coast, the high Andes make their closest approach to the Pacific Ocean. There, just twenty-two miles as the crow flies, is the high puna. Situated at over eleven thousand feet, the puna drops dramatically to the valleys below. Carved over the centuries into the steep, dry walls of the plateau by infrequent heavy rains is a maze of dangerously deep, breathtaking canyons, or *quebradas,* often leading vertically to the valley below. The scene is spectacular.

– – – – –

My desire to understand some of the gaps in my mother-in-law's story was the root reason why I was bouncing on a motorbike across some of the most desolate land imaginable.

Many months before, I had formulated a theory about Felipe that I wanted to verify with concrete evidence. I believed that in the early 1930s Carito's grandfather—facing personal disaster with the worldwide economic depression and the deaths of his only son and his wife—viewed the emerging gold rush in the western Sierra as an opportunity to rebuild his life and protect what he had worked for. So he relocated his new wife and young daughters to a place where he might pursue two tracks to prosperity. Poroto fit this model. In that small town he could reestablish himself as a merchant and businessman and at the same time explore opportunities in the gold fields above the town in the hills that bracketed the puna.

At the time the lure of gold drew hundreds of hopeful prospectors to the ridges on both sides of the Río Moche valley. The best mines were around Salpo. Other boom towns, including Haumachuco and Carabamba, also swelled with the flood of hopeful miners. Most of these hard men disappeared into the nearby hills and went to work carving out their claims.

It was a rough area for anyone to venture through. The single road to these towns, which wound up from the Moche Valley, was treacherous. Disagreements over claims, profits, or partnerships often flared into violence. Besides the inevitable geographic and transportation hazards, there were frequent robberies by some pretty bad men, and the roadblocks of shady government agents would chip away at the miners' profits. Still, the area drew hordes of men in search of fortune.

Felipe Lám was among these adventurous and intrepid men. I believe he judged the greatest problem to be the dangerous road up to Salpo and beyond. Few men escaped the bite of the highwaymen and corrupt government agents and the frequent accidents along that treacherous road. Cleverly, Felipe avoided the road and instead traversed the difficult ten miles from Poroto to his mine near Cerro Pingullo by mule train, up the impossibly steep walls of the canyons to the high puna.

The key to his plan may have been having people around him whom he could trust and rely on. Being new to Poroto and surrounded by others seeking their own fortunes—often at any cost—Felipe turned to men he knew and trusted, including his cousin Juan, who had also moved from Chepén in the north.

Felipe's small party gathered a few burros, loaded them with water and provisions, and set off on the track southward from Poroto. In doing so, they faced many challenges and dangers. The route followed a narrow path that hugged the canyon walls above the maze of deep quebradas that had been carved out of the dry earth. Eventually, after an exhausting journey, they arrived on the high, cold, windswept puna, where they established their rustic camp.

Since time began, people have named new places after familiar ones. These few men, all friends from Chepén, happy and proud to have successfully completed the difficult trek up into the puna, may have decided to call this new settlement Chepén after the place they all hailed from. Or perhaps the locals and indigenous people living nearby referred to the camp as "the men from Chepén." Either way, it seems like the name stuck.

## "No One Goes That Way"

In a spitting, cold, intermittent drizzle cast sideways by a brisk breeze, my *moto* driver and I abruptly pulled into a spacious green square, which was the heart of the pueblo of Chepén de Salpo. Juan stopped, leaned his bike over to let me tumble off, and shut down the shrill motor. He said, *"¡Estabas buscando Chepén—y ahora ya estás aquí!"* ("You were looking for Chepén—and now you are here!")

My last public transportation before beginning my walk.

All I had in my pocket was a single five-sol bill (worth about $1.75) and a single sol coin. I gave him the bill. Happy for the generous tip, Juan kicked his moto back to life and roared off, leaving me alone on the grassy plaza.

Wide open to the wind, the hamlet was, in a word, barren. The Spanish word *descampado* came to mind. It describes the place exactly: "in the open air; exposed to wind and weather; a wasteland."

At more than eleven thousand feet above sea level (the Pacific Ocean is only twenty-five miles away), Chepén de Salpo probably had a population of no more than two hundred people. While the grassy plaza was large, the hamlet itself was tiny and devoid of any evidence of frequent traffic. I sensed that little could be learned here about Felipe Lám. Still, there was a well-maintained church, a few houses, and a small school with a donkey grazing nearby. This and some adobe huts were all there was to the village.

The wind cut into me, and I was cold and numb. The light rain had soaked my short-sleeved shirt. I thought about my warm coat hanging on a chair in José's dining room and cringed.

Across the square I spied a couple of men sitting in the grass near the church, so I wandered over and introduced myself. I was invited to sit with them and accepted their offer of some coca leaves to chew. In halting Spanish I explained why I had come to Chepén.

I told them of my curiosity about their village and its origins and asked about the mines in the area. They didn't have much information for me on the village's history. But when I told them about my intent to venture down the trail to Poroto, one man, looking north, mumbled, *"Las profundidades"* ("The depths"). They then engaged in an excited discussion spoken too quickly for me to follow. They told me they knew of Poroto but had never been there. Few people in Chepén, it seemed, had ever been off the puna.

At that point an ancient-looking man, whom I guessed to be well past seventy, came up and introduced himself as Miguel. He described himself as a Puñero and explained that, at fifty-seven, he was the oldest resident in the village.

I again went through my speech, repeating to this village elder (only four years older than I) why I was there and what I was looking for. When asked about the town's history, Miguel told me that the community was established long ago by *extranjeros* (foreigners). At least that was what he had been told as a boy. He could not expand on this. *"Ahora ya no existen"* ("They are no longer here"), he said.

Regarding my walking to Poroto, Miguel assured me that it was indeed possible and that men had done it before. *"El camino a Poroto es fácil"* ("The trail to Poroto is an easy one"), he said. The men around him eagerly nodded in agreement. I was encouraged.

At this point I brought up Felipe's mines, Las Minas Casualidad. I asked if Miguel had ever heard of a place or a mine with that name.

*"No, nunca he oido de ese lugar"* ("No, I have never heard of this place"), Miguel said. He thoughtfully added, *"Pero en tiempos pasados creo que a veces la llamaban Casualidad por la dura vida."* ("But in the old days this place was sometimes called Casualidad because of the hard life here.")

One of the other men interjected that in the past many had come to the puna seeking fortune. *"Pero la mayoría a fracasado."* ("But most have failed.")

Ancient Miguel took over the conversation and somberly explained that almost no *gringos* ever came to Chepén and that certainly no one ever ventured into the areas below anymore. His entire tone seemed to change, as if by saying the trail was seldom used, he was cautioning me against using it. He went on, *"Porque, nadie va por allí...está muy peligroso."* ("No one goes that way...it is so dangerous.")

Then, contradicting himself, he said to me confidently, *"De todas maneras, una caminata a Poroto sí es posible y sin gran problemas—como de cinco a ocho horas, no más."* ("Still, a walk to Poroto is quite possible and should be no problem—only five hours, eight at the most.")

I asked about the mountain named Cerro Pingullo, alternately pointing to what I believed was the hill to the north and the one indicated on my map. The men showed no interest in my map and instead were unanimous that the hill I pointed to was not Cerro Pingullo. Rather it was a hill with no name. Cerro Pingullo, they agreed, must be somewhere farther to the west.

I questioned them about water along the trail to Poroto. Old Miguel

The village of Chepén.

told me that it would be *no problema* (no problem). The spring rains, he assured me, would provide plenty of water along the trail. He went on to say there was a good river farther down, along my path, and as I got closer to Poroto, there would even be small *tienditas* where I might buy provisions. *Hmm,* I thought, *only five hours…eight at the most. Water would be no problem. There would be plenty of water along the trail.* It sounded as if this would be easier than I had expected. I had actually hoped the walk would take me longer; I wanted to give myself plenty of time to enjoy the scenery and appreciate the landscape. *Eight hours—what kind of an adventure is that?*

We often hear only what we want to hear, and this was one such example. I heard "only five to eight hours" but somehow ignored the warning "No one goes that way because it is so dangerous." So I resolved to press on.

I conservatively figured on a full eight hours to make the walk. I felt confident that if I left right away, I could be in the valley and probably all the way to Poroto before dark. Even if I ran into delays, I should be able to secure lodging somewhere along the way.

— — — — —

About two weeks earlier, when Carito and I had arrived in Peru, we first stayed with her *tia* (aunt) Clara and *tio* (uncle) Carlos in Lima. Tia Clara, like Carito's mother, Evelina, is a strong woman of character and no stranger to life's difficulties. Her father, Juan, had immigrated to Peru from China with his cousin Felipe in 1908 and had also settled near Chepén in the north. According to Clara, her father was a compulsive gambler, and like many Chinese immigrants he smoked opium. Juan eventually squandered the family's wealth and had even lost his son, Clara's brother, on a gambling bet.

When I asked if she knew why Felipe—following the death of his first wife, Catalina—had moved his daughters and second wife to Poroto, she said she didn't know. However, her father, having lost everything he owned to gambling, had joined Felipe there. Clara was very young but recalled being Evelina's playmate in those days.

Tia Clara's recollections were helpful in piecing together the story of these bold men. She clearly remembered their talking about the mines and recalled that her father, with Felipe and several others, would often load their mules with supplies, foodstuffs, and water for journeys into the mountains. They would be gone for long periods of time. As children, she, Evelina, and their friends ran alongside the departing train of men and burros to the very edge of the village until the rising road diminished into a mere trail. There the men would say good-bye and send the children back home.

One thing Tia Clara said in passing, which I did not heed, was that she remembered the terrible condition the men were in when they returned from the canyons. She recalled their exhaustion and specifically the many cactus spines that plagued their skin.

When I explained my Felipe theory to Clara and mentioned my desire to someday retrace his journey, she looked doubtful.

*"¿Qué esperas encontrar?"* ("What do you hope to find?") she asked.

"I don't know, Tia," I responded. "Perhaps more information about his mines—whether the Chepén of the puna really is linked to the northern town of Chepén. I just don't know. I'm curious and looking for any connection."

*"Bueno, es posible"* ("Well, it's possible"), she said thoughtfully. *"Pero si vas, vas a necesitar un guía. Avísame como termina todo."* ("But if you go, you'll need a guide. Let me know how it comes out.")

# 5

# Into the Chasm

A friend loves at all times,
and a brother is born for a time of adversity.

—Proverbs 17:17

*Thursday, 3 November 2011, 1150 Hours,*
*Cabracay, La Puna Norte, Perú*
*(8° 07'11.79" S, 78° 40'56.48" W—Elevation 9,553')*

In life there are times and events we wish we could do over. In hindsight we often see that we ignored obvious warnings or signs that should have dissuaded us from whatever we did.

This was one of those times.

Proceeding beyond Chepén de Salpo at this point was really, really dumb. I should have turned around right then and gone back to Trujillo, but I didn't. Instead, I asked once again where the trail to Poroto started from the edge of the puna, and all four men pointed in the same general direction. I looked at my watch, saw that it was not yet noon, and verified that my bottle with almost two liters of water was secure in my bag. Again I found my knapsack was wet and remembered the broken bottle cap I'd discovered earlier. I needed to be careful and ensure the bottle was always upright.

Hefting my pack, I started off for the edge of the plateau. My dance with death had officially begun.

## Walk to the Edge

Leaving Chepén, where the terrain was quite level, I was able to establish a steady pace along the gently rolling landscape. The decreased oxygen at more than eleven thousand feet and the weight of my pack combined to help me quickly defeat the late-morning chill. Before long sweat glistened all over my body, and my shirt was damp. But my spirits were high, and I was thrilled to finally *really* be on my way.

Heading more or less northward along the winding track, I soon caught up with two weathered, middle-aged Indian women walking in the same direction. I moved wide to their right to pass them in a non-threatening way, but after I greeted them, they engaged me in a pleasant, although limited, conversation. They were naturally curious why I was there. Clearly, foreigners, especially strangely clad gringos, were seldom, if ever, seen here. In my halting Spanish I told them I was walking to Poroto.

"Where is Poroto?" one asked.

I pointed ahead, over the edge of the puna, and they both laughed

The barren plateau of the high puna.

and shook their heads. They commented quietly between themselves be-hind cupped hands in what I took for Quechua, the language of the Andean people. I understood none of it.

We walked side by side for some time. Along the way the rosy-cheeked, leather-skinned, and heavily clad ladies laughed easily, showing bright teeth and spectacularly pink gums, as I told them of my Peruvian-born wife and our three daughters. They said she was a lucky woman and then added that I was an even luckier man, which brought more laughter from them.

Nothing they said contradicted what I'd been told in Chepén about the trail over the edge of the puna or the location of Cerro Pingullo. And nothing gave me pause or reason to doubt that I was exactly where I should be and on the correct path. However, getting to the edge of the plateau and the trail took much longer than I'd expected.

After a while the two women peeled off on a narrow path to the east, nodding their heads, shyly waving, and giggling. Then it was quiet again, and I soon realized how much I missed their company.

But my solitude didn't last long. As I worked my way north and to the west of the hill, which the men in Chepén had told me certainly was *not* Cerro Pingullo, I became aware of several uniformed schoolchildren approaching me from behind. They seemed to have appeared out of no-where and were softly laughing and pointing at the strange sight ahead of them—a lightly clad gringo walking where, in their short lives, they'd probably never seen such a person before. I pretended not to see them and trekked on, occasionally glancing back at the cautiously approaching children, who ducked behind large boulders and giggled even more.

After a spell I came across a walled compound that enclosed the home of a local Puñero family. The schoolchildren, six in all, ran past me and spilled into the mud-walled yard. A tired-looking woman sat there, shucking beans and eying me suspiciously. I stayed outside the wall and asked if this was the trail to Poroto. She shook her head. I asked if she knew of Poroto, and she again wagged her head. Then a boy, about seven years old, came to me with a small jar of cloudy liquid and asked if I needed water. My bottle was down by just a third at this time, and I imagined how sick the untreated water would make me. With a small bit of disguised disgust and arrogance, I politely refused. *After all,* I told myself, *I'll be able to buy clean water in a few hours. No need to get the trots from some filthy farm water.*

I resumed my walk to the north and approached the edge of the chasm. The low, misty clouds had moved on, leaving a crystal-clear, dark-blue sky. I took a moment to look up and imagined I could almost see faint stars twinkling through the midday expanse above me. I then cautiously walked the last few dozen feet to the edge of the deep canyon, much as one approaches the railing of a high balcony. When I looked over the edge and saw the vast void splayed before me, the stunning view took my breath away. *Las profundidades* (the depths) was an apt description.

Behind me sat the table-like puna, bracketed by snowcapped peaks. On my left—to the west and a mere two dozen miles distant—was a flat gray haze that I knew was the Pacific Ocean. This is the closest the looming Andes mountains—4,300 miles long and the world's second-highest mountain chain—come to the coast.

But most spectacular was the amazing vista in front of me: a dramatic maze of a shattered landscape draped off the edge of the high plateau. These ancient ravines and canyons, or quebradas, were carved out of rock and sand by infrequent torrents of rains and were painted in a thousand shades of brown, ocher, and tan.

Somewhere down there, ten miles away, was my destination. I checked my map and compass and noted in the distance the hazy blue-gray blur of a distant valley, which I deduced was my target: Poroto.

I again checked my map and saw that the Puñero's compound, which I'd passed earlier, was perched at ninety-five hundred feet and was marked on my chart as Cabracay. It was set on the very edge of the puna. I had no idea what the name meant but realized these folks were certainly hearty. They had to be to endure the isolation, cold, and extremely windy

Here I began my descent into the spectacular canyons, las profundidades.

and dry climate. I wondered if Felipe and his colleagues, after struggling up the difficult trail from Poroto, had also reached this place called Cabracay and welcomed the water and shelter it may have offered.

Looking down, I contemplated my looming venture and drank heartily from my water bottle, which by now was nearly half empty. And I had not even started my descent!

I took one more compass reading and then carefully surveyed the hundreds of faint tracks below me. Among the web of trails were a couple that were more prominent. I was sure I would have no difficulty as long as I headed north and always downward.

## The Descent

The trail I chose seemed more heavily used than the others, and it headed in what I determined to be the direction I needed to go. As I set out, I found that, at first, the going was easy, but there was no escaping the precarious drop-off to my left. At some points the path was nothing more than a ledge carved from the side of a ravine. I had little chance to worry about the deep canyon below me as I concentrated on where I placed each uneven step, all the while dodging sporadic thorn-laced brush that ripped any bit of skin it touched.

The trail, covered with sand and crushed gravel-like debris, was initially smooth and well defined. But before long it grew more narrow and steep. After losing my footing a couple of times, I moved even more cautiously. A slip here could be a show-stopper.

The rugged landscape around me was mostly barren, but occasionally the route was lined with desiccated twigs and thorny bushes, all long dead. At times these became a problem as they closed in and forced me to weave in order to avoid the thorny arms that snagged my clothing or dragged against my arms, leaving a fine, stinging line of beads of blood.

It struck me how warm it had become since I'd started down the canyon wall. At first I welcomed the warmth, but before long, instead of shivering from the brisk wind racing across the high puna, I was sweltering in the still air of the quebrada. The temperature swing was dramatic, at least twenty to thirty degrees. I found myself uncomfortably hot and sweating in spite of a breeze gently rising from the deep valley below.

I soon came to a crudely constructed rock fence, placed at a point where the trail was carved into a sort of gully in the rocky hillside. The barrier included a sturdy iron grate secured with a heavy chain. While men with mules would be unable to pass through or around the barricade, I was able to toss my pack, lift myself over the obstacle, and drop heavily on my feet on the other side. Unknown to me at the time, in my scramble over the gate, my reading glasses—habitually perched on top of my head—fell off and were lost.

From that point on, the path got steeper. It's amazing how much effort it takes to walk downhill even with a light load on your back. I constantly had to restrain my body's weight against the pull of gravity, which was not easy considering how the crushed gravel and sand made the trail slippery. My exertions and profuse sweating made me increasingly thirsty. I had to stop frequently to catch my breath and take measured sips of water. I began to ration the size and frequency of my drinks. I needed my limited water supply to last until I got to the bottom of this canyon. Still, I was confident that in a few hours I'd have plenty of water to drink.

– – – – –

The day before I left Trujillo, the Peruvian papers were filled with the story of Ciro Castillo Rojo. He had become a household name and the topic of discussion in living rooms, cafés, and bars across the country. Ciro was an avid and experienced outdoorsman. He knew the region of the Colca Canyon near Arequipa in the south of the country and loved hiking there.

Six months earlier, in April 2011, while walking a well-established trail in southern Peru with his girlfriend, Ciro had fallen into a canyon hundreds of feet below. More than two hundred days later, his body was found at the base of a forty-six-hundred-foot cliff. It had taken sixty-five people thirty hours to retrieve his body and transport it to a nearby town for identification. The cause and details of his death were still a mystery when I began my adventure.

On the path to Poroto, I thought about Ciro and realized I didn't know these mountains and I was alone. If I fell off this mountain, my body might never be found.

Despite a tremor of apprehension, I continued on.

## My Feathered Companions

One reason I didn't stop and turn back was that I was really enjoying my hike. The view was spectacular, and the trail, while challenging at times, was not that difficult. I marveled at the diverse and ever-changing plant life along the path in that dry, seemingly dead place. But it was far from dead. So many varieties of desert plants were, amazingly, able to survive by clinging to the steep hillside.

On closer inspection I saw that many of the hardy plants were capped with small yellow, purple, red, or orange flowers. Most abundant was a scrub brush laced with thorns. These brittle bushes rose head high and occasionally crowded the trail, leaving only a low tunnel to navigate through. I soon understood the difficulty Felipe and his companions must have encountered as they struggled up this mountain: the impossibly steep climb, the unforgiving sun and heat, the thirst, and—not the least of all—these plants, all of which seemed to sport fierce spines and needles! It was as if they were competing to see which could be the meanest, sharpest, and nastiest!

Springtime had also brought out the best this foliage had to offer, with flowers and blossoms in the most unexpected places. Occasionally I also caught a glimpse of brown lizards sunning themselves before scampering off the trail, startled by my lumbering approach.

Before long I was joined by an amazing array of darting hummingbirds. Dozens of Andean Green-headed Hillstars (*Oreotrochilus stolzmanni*) swarmed and flitted around my head. These tiny creatures took turns hovering in place above my path. The experience was enchanting. The birds magically lingered inches from my face, cocking their tiny pointy-billed heads right and left, studying me carefully. Although I continued to move forward along the trail, the birds maintained their place about a yard in front and slightly above me.

At first I thought they were just curious, but when their dance continued for several minutes, I wondered if I was seen as an invader to their domain or if perhaps I was being warned of dangers ahead. My new friends stayed with me for about half an hour, and then, as quickly as they had appeared, they departed with a collective darting and twisting. The flock shot back up the side of the canyon. As I shuffled carefully along, I pondered the meaning of this weird and enchanting experience.

Descending the steep, rough trail, I noticed other hints of hidden beauty spread across the otherwise desolate landscape. There was no lush vegetation, but many types of cacti and brownish plants clung to the rocky, dry hillside. Most were brittle and appeared dead—until I looked closely at their stalks near the ground. There I saw faint, drab green streaks running up their tiny trunks, indicating a trace of life. These were patient living things awaiting the next rain shower.

One particularly interesting specimen was a squat cactus covered with millions of hairlike yellow spines, giving the plant a golden, glowing appearance, especially near the top. This fine coating concealed inch-long, gnarly, vicious spikes. I dubbed these plants "yellow tips." Some of them had bright reddish-purple tubular growths with crimson blossoms protruding from their tops. Beautiful! (I later learned that these are called *Oreocereus Celianus,* better known as the "Old Man of the Andes.")

## Across the "Crack of Fear"

Farther and farther I descended along the narrow path, if that is what it could be called. The trail became increasingly difficult to follow. There were no signs, no footprints to indicate the path had been used recently. Nonetheless, I was confident that down and more or less north was the right way to go. I continued to traipse along the steep canyon wall, all the while trying to keep my footing on the loose gravel and follow the frequently obscure track.

Before long my thighs ached and burned from the intense effort. I kept losing the trail as it disappeared into the thick, thorn-laced brush, only to emerge several yards above or beneath where I'd lost it. In my struggle to rejoin the trail, I was forced to move up or down the canyon wall, sliding on loose rock only to find again a telltale desiccated mule chip, which told me I was back on track.

Later in the afternoon, as the heat peaked, I came to a serious crack in the canyon wall and across the path—actually a dry gulch tumbling down a near-vertical crevice—which extended from the edge of the puna far above. A large rock was wedged into the narrow gully by scores of smaller rocks. The boulder was about two or three feet around, and if I was going to continue along the path to Poroto, I had no choice but to cross this precarious crack. I needed to step onto and over the large rock.

I did so gingerly, and as I shifted my weight—stretching to reach the other side—I felt and then heard a grinding, crunching sound. My heart sank as I felt the massive boulder shift below me and let loose with a roar. As the rock and a truckload of debris released into the canyon, I lunged over the instant void and fell hard on my knees on the other side, clawing for a handhold in the loose gravel and rock.

The boulder instantly disappeared, tumbling and crashing loudly down the gully and into the canyon below. Finally, with a huge thud it struck something hard and launched into the air, sailing out of sight. After what seemed like an eternity, but was actually just a few seconds, the ominous silence was shattered by another sharp report, followed by several others that loudly echoed from far below. The drop was too steep for me to see where the rock had finally landed.

I lay there for several moments, panting and terrified out of my wits, crouching on the edge of what was now a wide gap in the path behind me. I rested, sweating and wondering just how deep this canyon was. I was hot, dirty, and very thirsty. I took a drink from my bottle and was concerned to see how little water remained.

"Man! I am really looking forward to being off this mountain," I muttered.

– – – – –

For a few more hours, I worked my way along this precarious path. The heat was oppressive, but I was still optimistic and in fairly good spirits despite my near mishap with the boulder and the crevice.

By 4:30 p.m. I was almost out of water. It looked as though I had only two or three more swallows left, and the seemingly unending canyon still stretched far below me.

I was getting concerned about how little progress I was making down the canyon wall. Looking up to where I had started, my head spun at how high the canyon rim was above me. I was increasingly confused about how deep the canyon must be.

At this point I began to wonder if I would have to spend the night on the canyon wall. While it wasn't an appealing proposition, I wasn't overly concerned. Going back up the trail to the puna wasn't an option; there was that "small" problem of the huge gap in the trail left by the missing boulder.

I had yet to come across any level ground or suitable place to pitch a camp. But I was certain that even if I was forced to spend the night on the trail, it would only be a small inconvenience. *After all,* I thought, *a night on the mountain will just add to the exciting story I'll be able to tell once I get back home.*

## A Night in the Canyon

As the sun reached a point slightly above the canyon's wall, it was obvious I needed to find a place to camp for the night. I dropped my pack and checked my chart against my compass. That's when I discovered my reading glasses were missing. I am blessed with better-than-average sight at distances but helpless when it comes to reading or even seeing anything closer than arm's length. Rummaging through my survival gear, I found a small plastic magnifying glass, so I was able to study my map.

I was shocked to see just how little progress I had made. Unable to see anything outside the half-inch lens of the toy magnifying glass, I felt the first tightening of mild panic rising in my throat. I calmed myself by rationalizing that I needn't worry; I was only a few hours from my destination and just needed to continue down this trail to Poroto in the morning. I'd simply make camp along the trail, and by midmorning I'd be enjoying an empanada and a coffee in a Poroto café. No problem, right?

As I searched for a suitable place to make camp, I lost sight of the trail in the thick brush and found myself in a particularly tangled cluster of spiny thistle. Then I emerged on a small indentation in the hillside with a few feet of fairly level ground. Bingo! This would be my campsite and home for the night.

My crude campsite on the canyon wall.

I scraped away the larger rocks and brush. Using my best Boy Scout skills, I suspended my yellow plastic poncho between some dried brush to protect myself from any frost or dew. I then laid out my thin towel, and over it I spread my plastic, made-in-China solar blanket.

Satisfied and even proud of my temporary home for the night, I settled in. I drank heartily from the last cup of water in my bottle, leaving a few swallows for the morning. I whispered a quick prayer, thanking the Lord for this day and asking that he watch over me the next day when I completed my walk.

As I settled into my little nest, I looked over the vast panorama before me. As the day's last light faded, I watched the shadows of night chase the sun's fading rays along the opposite, eastward canyon wall. It was so quiet and stunningly beautiful. And soon very dark.

My last thoughts before I drifted off were of Felipe Lám. Eight decades before me perhaps he had camped on this spot with his mules and men and enjoyed the same beautiful views. Though I was totally exhausted and dangerously low on water, I was content and expected that tomorrow I would be sleeping in a comfortable bed.

Settling onto the hard spot on the rocks, I pulled my silver solar blanket up around my neck and drifted off to sleep.

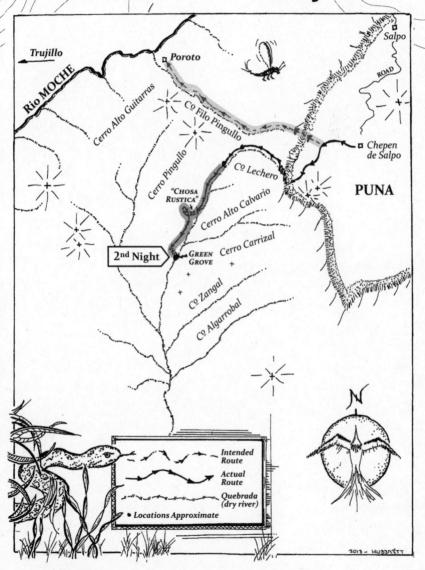

# 6

# Thirsty

Everybody's got plans…until they get hit.

—Mike Tyson

*Friday, 4 November 2011, 0500 Hours, North Side of Quebrada Barranca Blanca (White Canyon Gorge), Northern Perú (8° 07'22.07" S, 78° 42'03.30" W—Elevation 7,705')*

I woke early with a start. I was terrified. It was dark, and I was in a foreign place and very cold. In the faint dawn I saw a great void before me. I seemed to be hanging off the edge of the world, and the scene scared me to death.

The sun was not yet visible, and with the clear night the temperature must have dipped close to freezing, because there was a dusting of frost on my gear. Shrouded in darkness, I had to take a few moments to remember where I was. Then I realized I was awfully stiff.

I wasn't looking forward to removing the solar blanket, which to my surprise had proved effective in conserving my body's heat through the frigid night. How could such a hot place turn so cold overnight?

Then I noticed the silence. The stillness around me was unsettling. Not a thing stirred. I've never heard or felt such quiet. And I felt very alone. Yesterday's efforts had taken a toll on me. Every muscle and joint ached. I craved a drink of water, but after retrieving my battered water bottle, I was reminded how pitifully few sips were left.

As the sun slowly rose over the ridge above me, the sky morphed from black to midnight blue to indigo to a beautiful robin's-egg blue, speckled with occasional white clouds.

While I lay there beneath my thin cover, my head spun. At first I was afraid to move, fearing that I might tumble off the small landing into the canyon's depths.

Before long it was light enough to make out some small details, so I fumbled in my knapsack for the magnifying glass. With my small pen-light, I studied my map. Strangely, my compass indicated the canyon below me ran east and west. The night before it had run north and south—just as it should have, according to my map. I wondered if the compass had been damaged. I switched to my other compass and got a different reading. Which one was correct? Was either reliable?

My best guess was that the primary trail—the one I wanted to be on—was above me. If I could get up to that path, the subsequent descent into the Río Chepén valley should be pretty straightforward.

My attention drifted to the magnificent panorama appearing in the morning light. In the vast canyon below, the descent was so steep I

The canyon trails were narrow and treacherous.

couldn't see the bottom. An image projected on the facing canyon wall caught my eye. Then the shadows raced away from the emerging sunlight like birds in flight. The beauty of the moment captured me. I sat there dazed, soaking in the splendor of the retreating shadows. Mesmerized by the magnificent display, I watched and waited for the promised warmth of the rising sun.

## Back to the Trail

As I broke camp, I felt agitated, not only because of my questionable compasses and missing glasses, but also because of how little progress I had made the day before. If I was where I believed I was, I still had a good hike ahead of me to get to Poroto. What had begun as a five- to eight-hour stroll was looking more like a two-day trek. *I had better get started,* I told myself.

I packed my knapsack, gulped down the last few sips of my water, and set off, clawing my way up the hardscrabble hillside, looking for the trail. The tangled brush and cacti were thick, which made the going tough. The path, if there was one, was impossible to discern. As the sun rose, so did the temperature, and in no time I was sweating profusely.

After some slow progress I eventually came to a path that seemed to head in the direction I wanted to go. Back up on two feet, I was happy to be walking on a real path again. For a while the going was good. The trail gradually descended along the side of the canyon. The brush around me was high, and I saw burro tracks, with the accompanying old, desiccated dung, which seemed to be everywhere and nowhere at the same time. I was thirsty but had no water.

I admitted to myself I might really be in trouble.

– – – – –

Death by dehydration is a nasty process. Humans lose water via many outlets: sweat, urine, respiration, blood, and tears. Exertion, temperature, humidity, and a number of other factors also figure into the equation when trying to determine how long a human can survive without water. Dehydration is first evidenced by thirst, headaches, and cracking of the tongue and lips. Later, the symptoms include persistent skin irritation, abdominal pain, a swollen tongue, and hallucinations. All indicate a person is in serious trouble.

The amount of water required daily for optimal health is about two liters (slightly more than two quarts). However, this amount increases dramatically as a person exerts himself or as the temperature rises.

In *How to Survive Anything, Anywhere,* Chris McNab explains how important water is for survival:

> Urine output alone counts for approximately 1.5 liters of water lost per day. Defecation uses 0.2 liters and sweat/skin diffusion releases 0.5 liters. As a general rule, each person of average build, living in a temperate climate and going about their normal activity, will lose about 2–3 liters of body fluids each day. Even if he lay in bed for 24 hours, he would still lose about 1 liter. These figures climb dramatically under conditions of high temperature, illness (particularly vomiting or diarrhea), injury or physical exertion. In tropical heat, for example, an individual can lose up to 4 liters of water per day through perspiration alone, and someone working hard in desert conditions during the daytime could require up to 25 liters of drinking water per day.
>
> Losing one-tenth of the total body water content results in serious illness, including headaches, dizziness, shaky limbs, blurred vision and difficulty breathing. If the proportion of body fluid lost goes beyond one-tenth, the individual goes into circulatory shock and is likely to die if the fluid equation is not quickly balanced.[1]

The drier the climate, the more acute these factors become. At a temperature of 85 degrees Fahrenheit, if a person is resting in the shade, the maximum number of days that person can survive without water is seven or eight. At 120 degrees in the shade, the estimated survival time is about two days. Again, heat and physical exertion greatly accelerate these equations. As a rule of thumb, most people would die after three to four days in the shade without water. That's our *limit*. When exerting ourselves, or in an extremely hot climate, this limit diminishes dramatically.

- - - - -

The bottom line was that water had rapidly risen to the top of my life-priority scale. I wished I had taken the offered *taza* of water from the young Puñero at Cabracay. *Why didn't I?* I asked myself. If only I had known what was ahead. I clearly remembered that little guy offering me his cup of cloudy water and how *I*—the privileged *norteamericano*—had brushed him off by saying I had enough of my own.

Weighing my options, I knew my only choice was to continue down that canyon wall and to my destination as quickly as possible.

## Isolated

I saw absolutely no trace of human beings around me. I was in the most remote place I had ever been. When I was in the military, stationed in the Arabian Desert, I had seen some isolated places; however, I'd never felt as far removed from human contact as I did now. There were no roads, no wired power poles, or hilltop antennas. My sole link to any life form was donkey droppings, indicating a recently traversed trail. I followed these little piles, figuring the beasts had been serving some men traveling through this mountain. Why else would burros be here? Then it occurred to me that, while I saw numerous faint mule tracks, I had not seen even one accompanying human footprint.

Nonetheless, I tried to remain positive. I believed that in a few hours I would surely be in Poroto or some settlement near there. I had no choice but to keep moving.

- - - - -

About this time I was getting pretty buddy-buddy with God. Other than a few quick prayers the day before, I had hardly given the Lord a thought. But now, realizing I might have miscalculated the difficulty of this journey, I knew I needed help. I was hot, thirsty, cut, and banged up. I began praying for God's intervention.

The trail I was following wormed farther along the steep canyon side and appeared to be a primary track. For a while it presented a comfortable descent, working its way more or less horizontally along the north side of the deep quebrada. Occasionally I could look down and glimpse the dry arroyo far below, littered with boulders and rocks. From what I could judge, it had been some time since water had flowed through the rugged gulch, and when it did, it was no doubt a torrent washing away debris and smoothing the stone hillsides along its banks.

I made good progress and after a bit spied a prominent outcropping clinging to the canyon wall. Perched upon it was something resembling a structure. At first I wasn't sure what it was, but I was happy to see that my route would take me that direction. "Thank you, God! Thank you!" I prayed out loud as I picked up my step and worked my way toward what I hoped might be a settlement or even a home…hopefully with some water.

## La Choza Rustica

In time the path led me to an abandoned settlement perched on a semi-level outcropping. It turned out to be a *choza,* an ancient low-walled adobe shack. The walls of the hovel were only three or four feet high, and the interior was full of debris and litter. There was no sign of recent habitation.

I wondered about the people who had built and lived in this place. Perhaps they were shepherds seeking shelter from the sun or nighttime cold. A place like this would have provided some refuge from the wind and sun during the day as well as shelter and warmth through the cold nights. The hut's crude thatch roof had collapsed long ago, and plants had grown up and died inside and all around the dwelling.

Common sense told me that human settlements need water and are usually chosen for their proximity to its source. Building this place had taken a lot of effort, and the inhabitants had needed water to stay here for any length of time. I searched around the dwelling for a water source, a well or a spring, but found nothing. The settlement was bone dry and in a shambles. *Kinda like me,* I thought.

Although it was early morning, I was hot, exhausted, and *so* thirsty. I looked to the place from which help was most likely to come—my Lord—and I prayed, *God, throw me a bone here!* I knew I had blundered big-time and really needed him to step in. I fervently asked for help. This was my lowest point so far.

I could not escape the blazing heat. Sitting under the clear blue sky, the sun beating down on my head, I again struggled with my tiny magnifying glass to study my map. I worked to orient my compass to my chart and determine where I was, but it was all very confusing.

I noticed on my map two possible positions indicated by small black squares. One was named La Cuchilla (the razor), which was about where I thought I was. The name seemed appropriate to the sharp outcropping where the old choza sat. But, according to my map, it was on the wrong side of the canyon I believed I was in. The other place, called Tayal, was a cluster of at least six structures and was much too large and too far north from my supposed location. Actually, neither location seemed right, and I ended up with more questions than answers. That worried me.

Absent any shade and sitting next to this dilapidated hut, I pleaded with God, *Please, Lord, guide me off this mountain!* Then I waited for some kind of answer, trying to ignore my pounding heartbeat. The answer I received was absolute silence. Nothing moved, not a breath of a breeze or a bird or a lizard. It was as if time and motion and life all stood still. I felt as if I were the only living thing in a dead world. I'd never experienced such silence or loneliness. It all was so lifeless that I checked to see if I was still breathing.

I looked once more for some source of water, and after a bit of kicking around in the debris, I decided to move on. I selected what I hoped was my best option among the scores of faint trails leading away from the old settlement. Working slowly along the steep mountainside, I was forced to move more cautiously, picking my way along the even steeper trail. In places the path disappeared among large areas of loose rock and gravel that had slid down the canyon wall. I came to a place where the ground above me had given way. I had to crawl on all fours across the field of loose debris.

Finally, after creeping across another dangerous stretch, I rested and struggled to catch my breath through dry, cracked lips. Looking down into the quebrada, I saw the remains of a badly decomposed burro about a hundred feet below. What remained of its face looked up at me and seemed to be laughing, its generous teeth exposed in a permanent smile. The carcass was contorted, wrapped around a massive boulder. The poor creature faced me belly up, apparently having tumbled off the precipice until the boulder checked its fall and broke its back. The *gallinazos* (buzzards) first visited the animal's remains, and they were followed by flies and ants and any number of other insects. Finally millions of parasites, flesh-eating bacteria, and microbes had begun to finish the job. All that remained of the poor animal was a skeleton covered by a torn and shredded bag of hide, perforated by sun-bleached ribs. Seeing the demise of this surefooted and hardy animal, I realized pointedly that I was in a very perilous place.

I turned away and again weighed which of the scores of trails crisscrossing the canyon's wall I should take. From a distance these meandering, fishnet-like game trails and burro paths, beaten through the brush, seemed like a maze. I was worried and wanted nothing more than to be off that hill. I was hurting, hot, and oh so thirsty. I needed help, the sooner the better. I repeatedly looked to heaven and boldly and loudly pleaded with God to save me. Still no response. Nothing.

Overcome with sadness, I hefted my pack and resolved to move on. My sack, even though it held just a few items, felt heavier than ever. Negotiating the path was exhausting; I knew I was using massive amounts of calories and fluids, probably working harder physically than ever before. My clothing was soaked with sweat, and my heart pounded. I knew this stress on my body could not continue much longer. But I had no choice except to keep going.

Another daunting crevice forced me to crawl on my hands and knees to cross it. I had to grasp roots and thorny brushes to keep from sliding away. My hands were torn, and I often frantically bicycle-kicked for a foothold. Panting to catch my breath, I took a brief break. I was covered in dust and had cuts all over my legs and arms.

As I pressed on, the trail would frequently disappear, and I would aim for another path on the other side of yet another treacherous crevice. Below me was a really steep and frightening drop-off. I halted, my entire body shaking uncontrollably. Was this from fear of almost tumbling down the gulch or something more sinister?

This shaking was horrible. I was despondent and for the first time believed I might not make it off the mountain alive.

I noticed I had stopped sweating, which wasn't a good sign. My breathing was shallow, my head was spinning, and, most disturbing of all, I actually felt chilled as I sat in the desert sun.

I *had* to find some water.

# 7

# The Green Grove

The pride of your heart has deceived you,
    you who live in the clefts of the rocks
    and make your home on the heights,
you who say to yourself,
    "Who can bring me down to the ground?"

—Obadiah 1:3

*Friday, 4 November 2011, 0900 Hours, Far Above Quebrada Barranca Blanco (White Canyon Gorge), Las Profundidades (The Depths), Northern Perú*
*(8º 07'19.23" S, 78º 42'48.35" W—Elevation 7,734')*

With care and difficulty I made it across the next narrow gulch, but once on the other side, I realized I was in an even more precarious place.

Beneath me was a mass of loose gravel and crumbling stone. Again I kicked and clawed my way across, looking for any possible anchor. There just weren't any decent handholds or footholds. I'd grab at brittle thistle, which then uprooted, forcing me to claw into the stony soil. Below me was an almost vertical drop and ahead was more of the same. I realized I had made a big mistake in choosing this path.

My legs were shaking, my back was cramping, and my heart seemed to be beating through my chest. I was beginning to fall apart. I feared imminent disaster.

Finally I found a relatively safe spot to stop and rest. I fell back and tried to catch my breath. When I revived somewhat, I surveyed my situation and did a damage assessment. I knew I was in a bad spot. Below me was a deep, threatening gulch that swallowed any sand or rocks I kicked into its mouth. I examined my arms: a red mass of cuts and scrapes. The oozing wounds presented a plethora of leaking body fluids. Whenever I stopped moving, swarms of flies and gnats had a feast on the sudden source of liquid sustenance, swarming to my ripped flesh, fighting one another for sips of the life-giving fluid.

As thirsty as I was, I wished I were like them. How did these creatures manage to survive in this harsh environment without some food source like me coming along? Where did they find *their* water?

I turned again to God. *Hello, God, me again,* I prayed. *What do you recommend?* My sarcasm was answered with more silence. I was immediately embarrassed and ashamed of my irreverence and went on to wholeheartedly pray for my rescue, for some help.

Again the answer was silence.

Matthew 7:7 says, "Ask and it will be given to you." Well, believe me, I was asking. Man, was I asking! I was pleading, begging! Bring on some receiving!

It was obvious that any further advancement beyond the dangerous gully was futile. I knew I'd have to return to the choza and find another route. But there was no way I could retrace the dangerous path I had just traversed. I had to find another way back. Looking down, I knew I could not maneuver over or around the cliff. My only option was to go up, but I really had no desire to try that. I was exhausted and doubted I could make it. Of course, I told myself, considering my options, I could just sit right there and die.

Or I could climb up.

- - - - -

My compass indicated I was heading northeast instead of north—nearly opposite of the direction I wanted to go. I was perplexed, but I knew what

I had to do. I had to climb that hill and find a better way to return to the choza.

Through cracked lips I whispered a quick prayer, asking for strength and wisdom. "God, please guide me through this obstacle. You are in control. I hope you have a plan, because I don't." Then I once again hefted my pack and pushed off, clawing on my hands and knees, straight up the hillside through the worst tangled thickets and thorns I had yet seen. There was no trail, so I had to make my own. The effort was grueling, and my progress was slow. I paused again and again to catch my breath. The soil was loose and frequently gave way beneath me, causing me to slide backward and lose ground.

I was panting from the altitude, exertion, and lack of water. Each time I stopped, I sat on my haunches, gasping for breath and wishing I was anywhere but here. Below me was an almost vertical drop and ahead awaited more of the same—hard going.

– – – – –

On one stop to rest, I perched on a large, sharp rock and again assessed my options. After a while I glanced up at a small patch of soft dirt above me and saw something that sent chills through my overheated body. In the soft dry soil was a well-defined and obviously fresh paw print of a cat—a *very big cat*.

There are only two cats native to this region of Peru: the pampas cat (*Leopardus colocolo* or *Leopardus pajeros*) and the similar bobcat-sized Andean mountain cat (*Leopardus jacobita*). This paw print was probably from the Pampas cat, as it is much more common in this area. It really didn't matter; either way *something* else was out there with me, and it, too, was hungry, thirsty, and competing for the same limited resources. I added this new revelation to the growing list of things that, given the chance, could hurt or kill me.

So with God in my thoughts and a prayer nearly nonstop on my lips, I pushed farther up the hillside. Every ten or twenty feet I had to stop and catch my breath, and when I did, swarms of flies attacked me. *Where did they come from?* Nearly two hundred feet up the hillside, I finally came to a faint trail leading toward the choza. After about two hours of wasted time and energy, I staggered back, exhausted, into the abandoned settlement.

## Back at the Choza

My little excursion across the dangerous gully, along the wrong trail and back, had used up precious time and body fluids. It was late morning, and already the sun and heat were unrelenting. I was severely dehydrated and knew I was in serious trouble. I sat on a rock, feeling completely defeated and thought, *Wasted time, wasted energy, and, worse, wasted fluids!* I was demoralized. I hated that mountain! I hated myself for being in this position, for thinking this would be a simple, short hike in the hills. *How could I have been so stupid?* I had no one to blame but myself. If I could have cried, I would have, but there simply was no fluid for tears left in me.

Sitting in the hot sun, I realized I was back at square one. I needed to find a way off that rocky outcrop, so I took several compass readings and struggled to orient my map. Things just did not make sense. I recognized that the heat and thirst were impeding my judgment. Besides the handicap of having to use the small magnifying glass, my compass readings were bizarre. What was west a few hours earlier was now northwest. With the late-spring sun high and almost directly overhead, it was no help in my deciphering which direction I was heading.

Staggering around the perimeter of the old settlement precariously perched on the outcropping, I spied what looked like a trail leading down to what I believed was the west. It seemed to be the trail I wanted and should have been on all along. I felt I needed to go that way, and as tired as I was, I immediately set off toward the trail.

*Lord Jesus, please help me,* I prayed. I was confident that God heard my cry. I only hoped that when his answer came, I would be able to recognize it.

I headed off the razorback ridge where the choza was perched and loped toward three distinct saddleback hills ahead of me, which according to my chart should have been my target. I proceeded carefully, feeling very lightheaded. At times I forgot what I was heading for, a sign I was getting critically dehydrated. I slowly made my way around the ever-steeper hillside until I realized it was impossible to proceed any farther. The trail was not clear after all. A deep and impossible gulch stood between me and my target. I needed to get to those three saddleback hills in the distance, but they were still unreachable. I had to backtrack once again.

## A Patch of Green Below

As I staggered along the trail, I looked down into the canyon. There, far below, I spotted a small green patch in the otherwise brown and gray terrain. Green? Green meant life! All vegetation needed water, and in this desolate place water equaled life. Water! There had to be water somewhere in that deep quebrada.

I knew what I had to do. It was my only hope. In order to survive I resolved to somehow go down into the deep canyon and find the life source of this greenery. I had not eaten in two days, but that was far from my primary concern. *I needed water!* Finding water was my first and only priority. There was no other choice.

It was already early afternoon when I started down the steep slope toward the green grove below. Descending, I had only thorny bushes and an occasional cactus to provide a handhold or foothold to keep me from sliding. With each tentative step I was totally committed to reaching the canyon bottom. I had no idea how—or if—I would ever be able to climb back out. I didn't care. I had to have water.

On the way down the steep incline, as my foot scraped the surface, the long, gnarly spines of a large, dried-up cactus pierced my soft shoe and riddled my foot. A few of the hairlike spines went completely through the edge of my foot, and I would have vomited with the pain if I'd had any fluids in me. *What else could go wrong?*

As I gingerly took off my shoe, several of the thin spines embedded in my foot broke off. I fished some duct tape from my bag and used it to draw out some of the splinters. I then wrapped my foot with the remaining tape. When the stinging diminished, I painfully replaced my shoe and continued slipping down the slope as best I could.

Now I was even more careful to move as slowly as possible. Even so I could not avoid more brushes with the thorn-laced bushes and cacti. Everything from the larger, vicious, daggerlike spines to the tiny hairlike ones pierced my flesh through my soft shoes and thin pants and shirt. At one point my head lightly brushed against a plant, and I soon found several spines painfully impaled in my scalp.

After an exhausting and dangerous eighteen-hundred-foot descent, which took about an hour and a half, I finally reached the bottom of the quebrada. I was ripped up, parched, and exhausted. The last few feet to the dry riverbed were a sheer drop, and not caring what I fell on, I plunged, landed heavily, and rolled to a stop. I felt completely spent.

After resting in that canyon-like arroyo for maybe a half hour to catch my breath—with my heart pounding and my head spinning—I tried to gather myself. I looked downstream, and there, perched on a rock about fifteen feet from me, was a large *viscacha*—a fat, long-tailed, Andean cousin of the chinchilla. The creature took one look at me and scampered off into the mass of large boulders strewn throughout the dry arroyo. The small rodent didn't represent a source of meat or nutrition. I wasn't hungry—*I was thirsty.* I thought of the fluids pulsing through its small body and imagined that if I could capture it and kill it, I would squeeze the rodent's tiny body and drink any fluids that might ooze out of it.

But I was too beat up and weary to have any chance of chasing down the little creature in this maze of rock and vicious plant life.

## Looking for Water

I had hoped to find water, but instead of being the flowing brook I had envisioned, the streambed surrounding me was bone dry. I was miserably disappointed.

When I had looked from the choza high above, this grove had appeared so lush and green. My thirst had seduced me. The descent had been painful and exhausting. Now I feared it also had been futile. Close up I saw that the green stalks were actually a drab green-brown color and covered with dust. I suspected these plants had not seen water in a long time.

After a short rest I shrugged off my pack and climbed over several huge boulders, working my way through masses of thorny gray vines. Eventually I was able to reach the bamboo-looking thicket. My first hope and thought was that water might be stored in the stalks of these tall plants. I took out my knife and sawed through a nearby stalk until I had a long section free. After sawing away, I was able to pierce the plant's hard center and tip it up to my mouth and...*nothing*. It was bone dry. *So much for that.*

Crawling on my belly, I continued deeper into the grove, working my way as far as I could go into the palisade of hard, dry stalks. I sought the lowest point in the streambed, knowing from my air force survival training that if there was any water, that's where it would be. I crawled about a hundred feet through the parched, crackling bed of dead leaves and stalks until I finally arrived at what seemed the lowest point in the streambed.

Then, like a dog, I dug.

At first the soil was soft, but after about a foot, it became rocky and much more difficult to claw through. It reminded me of the hard, crusty caliche I've had to pickax through in Texas. As I worked through the stony soil, I imagined the dirt was becoming slightly moist. Encouraged, I pulled out my jackknife and used it to speed my digging.

*Could it be true?* I thought. Then I imagined I could feel welcomed humidity rising from the hole and into my face. I eagerly pressed on. I hoped against hope that, like a hole scooped out at the beach, my crater would fill with water. It didn't.

After digging through nearly two feet of hard, rocky soil, I realized that it was becoming ever so slightly damp. I paused for a moment and waited for the hoped-for trickle of water to moisten the pit. Nothing happened.

Still, I was sure I felt a slight dampness in the very deepest part of the hole and continued my frantic excavation. Even though the pit failed to fill with the sweet spring water I envisioned, I hoped for a miracle. I dug deeper.

Taking a short break, I looked around me. Maybe there was a better spot to dig. There was none. I was at the lowest point of the dry cane bed. Discouraged, I waited some more. Then with the afternoon light fading, I climbed out of the thicket and worked my way back over the thorny, vine-covered boulders and returned to my knapsack in the riverbed.

Collapsing to my knees, exhausted and parched, I said to no one, "What do I do now?"

# 8

# Sick

Let's rise and be thankful, for if we didn't learn a lot
today, at least we may have learned a little. And if we
didn't learn even a little, at least we didn't get sick. And
if we did get sick, at least we didn't die. So let us all be
thankful.

—Leo F. Buscaglia, *Born for Love: Reflections on Loving*

I'm sick of following my dreams. I'm just going to ask
them where they're going and hook up with them later.

—Mitch Hedberg

*Friday, 4 November 2011, 1515 Hours, At the Bottom of Quebrada
Barranca Blanco (White Canyon Gorge), Northern Perú
(8° 08'20.32" S, 78° 42'37.60" W—Elevation 5,620')*

I had to figure out something. Quickly! I was in bad shape, and nightfall
was not far away. I knew I was completely lost, deep in an obscure canyon, and in serious jeopardy. I was thirsty and out of water. No one knew
where I was. No one was coming for me. Despair enveloped me like a
heavy cloak.

When the eventual spring floods came, my desiccated body would
be flushed down this rocky canyon, perhaps wrapped around a rock like
the burro I'd seen earlier, my teeth smiling up at nothing in particular.
Would my remains ever be found?

I had no fight left in me and prayed desperately, *Lord! Please tell me.*

*What do you want me to do?* I wept dry tears and cried out, "Is this how you want me to die? What have I done? Have I been that bad? Am I that bad?"

I heard nothing in reply. Only punishing silence.

## Sucking Silt

Suddenly I had an idea. I rummaged through my knapsack and collected the single pair of clean underwear I had brought with me. With fleeting energy I staggered and crawled once more back over the thorn-laced boulders, into the cane grove, on my belly, returning to the hole I'd dug. I saw it still had not filled with water. In fact, it no longer felt faintly damp.

I dug deeper and gathered a small handful of slightly moist clay, put it into my skivvies, and wound the cloth tightly around the clump of dirt, twisting and squeezing it ever tighter. Just as I had hoped, a few beads of brown moisture appeared on the surface of the underwear. I was ecstatic! Eagerly I licked the brown dribbles of silty, chalky fluid and was startled by how foul it tasted. Still, it was moisture, and I sucked on the fabric. I gathered another clump of soil and then another, repeating the process again and again. While this did little to quench my thirst, my dry, cracked lips and mouth welcomed the dampness.

Each time I coaxed only a few spoonfuls of bitter fluid from my makeshift filter to my waiting mouth. Almost none of the small amount of liquid made it past the parched tissue in my mouth and throat to the rest of my body, where I needed it most.

I rolled onto my back and cried out through the towering plants above me, "Lord Jesus, help me! I'm so sorry for all my sins. Please, God, please help me!" I had never felt so low, and I wept uncontrollably.

Broken, I again negotiated the painful track over the boulders and thorn-laced vines to my pack in the riverbed. I was too tired to make a camp and simply dropped into a rocky patch between two boulders and passed out.

– – – –

About an hour after drinking the muddy water, I was stirred awake by a wholly unpleasant feeling. I tried to stand and was swiftly crippled by severe stomach cramps. Then uncontrollable diarrhea racked my gut, and I doubled over, barely able to drop my pants before the eruption. All I could think of was, *No! More fluid lost!* It took a while before I could stand upright again. The episode drained absolutely everything out of me.

From my experience and training, I knew that any hope of survival came down to the basic element of water. I could find shelter; I could easily make a fire if I needed to. Although there was hardly anything edible around me, I knew I could find food and subsistence if I had to. But at this point, water was the key to my survival. Three days is the limit for anyone. I knew that the average person—a resting person—could go without fluids in this heat for about three days. Factoring in the extreme exertion I had been subjecting my body to, I reckoned my time was diminishing quickly. Perhaps my time had run out. I was indeed in dire straits. Without some kind of intervention, I wasn't going to survive!

As I thought about my predicament, I remembered the story of Jesus's disciples caught in a horrific storm on the Sea of Galilee and how Jesus did not immediately come to their rescue. Throughout the night the disciples rowed hard toward their destination, yet they found themselves ever farther from it. They were on a dangerous sea, seemingly alone, and in mortal danger.

Even when the Lord revealed himself to them, he did not immediately come to their aid. Instead, he waited for them to call upon him.

I, too, found myself in a sea—one of rock, burned earth, and dangerous terrain. I was thirsty and adrift—hopelessly lost. I called upon the Lord to save me, and he waited. I made known to him what I wanted, what I needed, and he still waited. I pleaded, bartered, cursed, and begged. And he waited.

I knew I was in way over my head. How often do we find ourselves in a situation or an environment that, at the outset, we felt competent or even expert enough to handle, only to realize later that we are beyond our limits?

I thought about how God did not let his disciples perish in that storm on the Sea of Galilee. All they had to do was call out to him, acknowledge him, and have faith in *him*. That story gave me hope.

God had not led me into the wilderness to test me. Nor was he punishing me. God gives us freedom. I believe God allowed me to follow my selfish desires, my prideful arrogance, thus getting myself into trouble. Prior to this ordeal, I had countless opportunities to walk in *his* path, but too often I was busy following my own route, and, sadly, too often I put God in the backseat. God knew of my boastfulness, strong will, and pride, and *he* gave me an opportunity to seek *him* and follow *his* ways. This was simply another chance for me to draw closer to *him*.

I had developed what the Bible calls a "stiff neck" and needed a serious wake-up call.[2] The Lord knew that in order for me to fully appreciate his power and authority, I needed to *feel* his grace and physically *experience* his blessings. He knew that a complete humbling would compel me to submit and accept *his* will.

I prayed again.

## Putting My World Map to Use

Ever since I was young, I have been fascinated with maps. As a result, I have accumulated a pretty good collection of them. I remember riding my bicycle from the east side of San Jose, California, to the H. M. Gousha map company on the Alameda in the downtown area. There I would peer through the plate-glass window and into the map room as the cartographers hand-painted watercolors and filled in details of their popular road maps. I was transfixed.

Yet, in the end a map is basically a large piece of paper, and I definitely had a need for some paper. When my stomach cramped again, followed by another attack of raging diarrhea, I was better prepared. I had pulled out my beautiful full-color National Geographic world map and made a quick study of countries I could do without. *Iran. Yeah, Iran will be the first lucky one,* I decided. I tore out a rough square from the paper map and used it where I now most had a need. Within minutes Central Asia joined the ranks. Then more waves of cramps racked my body, doubling me over. I no longer had time to worry about any particular geography. Quickly vast areas of the Pacific Ocean were torn out to aid the cause. Within minutes the polar regions were gone, even as I longed for the imagined water and coolness they portrayed. All in all, it was a pretty unpleasant situation.

Time passed. After a while I saw in the dry riverbed farther downstream the tops of more green plants. *Water flows downhill,* I thought. *Maybe there'll be water there.* Slightly reenergized and taking care to avoid the land mine–like cactus plants that carpeted the riverbed, I stumbled over the boulders in that direction.

It took me about half an hour to reach the green-gray grove downstream, wedged into a narrow point of the canyon. Again I discovered that the bases of the stalks were bone dry, and to my disappointment the soil around them was even drier than at the first grove.

From the depth of this new despair, I again petitioned God for my physical salvation. *Lord! Help me!* I cried. Thoroughly demoralized, I grabbed my pack and headed back upstream. Along the way I began to throw out some weighty, now useless items. The bulky and cherished paperback *The Winds of War* went first.

The shadows of dusk were swiftly appearing in the deep canyon, and I returned once more to the hole I had dug. It was still dry. Ignoring the terrible toll the drops of clay-tinged water had caused earlier, I again gathered some clay and squeezed it through my shorts, sucking at the brown beads of moisture. I had no other choice. Thirst drove all my actions. I dug even deeper and scooped up a few more handfuls of damp clay and repeated the process. I didn't care how sick this would make me.

Sure enough, before long, waves of diarrhea again racked my body.

Parts of China disappeared, followed by Siberia. My National Geographic chart was shrinking fast.

*At this rate the world won't last long. Nor will I.*

- - - - -

Sprawled on the canyon floor, I had little energy to move. But my heart was pounding so hard I couldn't think clearly. I was at a loss as to what to do next. The smallest effort made me breathless, and I found myself panting in shallow, dry gasps. I wanted so badly to be back home in Texas with my wife—mi vida—and my three wonderful daughters. *What am I doing here? Why? Why have I done this?* I asked myself over and over.

I was dying. This was a new experience for me, and in a somewhat twisted way, I found it fascinating to watch, as though I were outside myself, an observer watching a man die.

Then a realization came flooding back to me: No one knew where I was. No one would know how I passed my last hours or what had happened to me. All they would know was that I had simply disappeared.

I felt guilty and utterly alone.

Not long afterward I felt the urge to urinate and quickly fished a scrap of plastic from my bag. Leaning against a rock, I deposited the small bit of fluid into the plastic and lifted it to my lips. The disgustingly pungent and sour taste brought me no relief. It was another futile exercise. *So it has come to this, has it?* I asked myself.

In survival school the instructors hammered into us the dangers of drinking urine. We were told stories of shipwrecked survivors who resorted to drinking their own waste, which only accelerated their demise. "Never, never do it!" they told us.

Despite that, here I was, in desperation, doing just that.

I fell prostrate to the dirt. I knew I was defeated, completely beaten down. I cried out in prayer, "Lord, you know what I want. I've been asking all day! Please, please, Lord Jesus, tell me—what do you want of me? Show me, Lord! Show me. Tell me! I don't know what else to do!"

I was an utterly broken man. "Do you hear me, God?" I cried out through my parched throat. And then I added, wailing to the canyon walls, "You win!"

After lying in that dry Andean riverbed a few minutes—filthy, parched, and drained of hope—I again turned to God, this time calmly and soberly. Instead of asking for deliverance, I said, "Jesus, you know what I want. What is it you want of me, Lord? Is this where you want me to die? Is this how?" I knew he was aware of my needs; in fact, I believed he knew them before I even asked. Still, no answers came to my prayers and pleas.

As is my tendency, I had been doing a lot of talking but not much listening. I wondered, *What is God telling me? Is it his intent that I die here, in this forlorn place?*

Then I came to what I now believe was the turning point. I prayed out loud, "God, if this is what you want, so be it. I surrender. I accept your will. You know what I want, but, Lord, you know what's best for me. I accept your will. Whatever you want, Lord, I'm on board."

A great peace came over me after that prayer. I was physically exhausted, out of water, and out of options. I was defeated but at peace.

In my humbled and broken condition, I realized it didn't matter so much what *I* wanted. God knew what my destiny was. We will all perish. Perhaps this was my time. I then accepted God's will, whatever it was, without conditions.

My last words mumbled that night summed it all up: "You're the boss, Lord."

Then, lying there in the warm sand of that deep quebrada as the shadows of the rapidly descending dusk engulfed the canyon, I fell quickly and soundly to sleep.

# Day 3

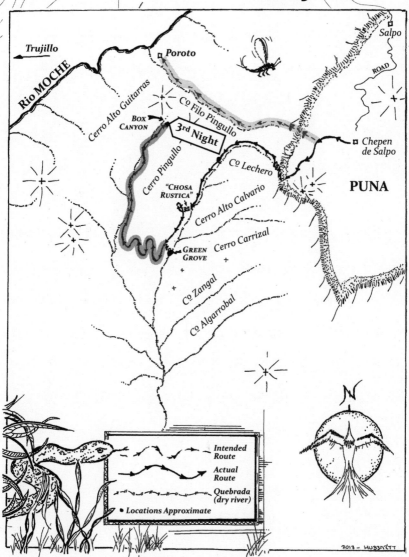

Trujillo ←

Rio MOCHE

Poroto

Salpo

ROAD

Cerro Alto Guitarras

Co Filo Pingullo

BOX CANYON

3rd Night

Chepen de Salpo

Cerro Pingullo

"CHOSA RUSTICA"

Co Lechero

PUNA

Cerro Alto Calvario

GREEN GROVE

Cerro Carrizal

Co Zangal

Co Algarrobal

N

Intended Route

Actual Route

Quebrada (dry river)

• Locations Approximate

2013 – HUBBNETT

# 9

# "Hey, Scott. You Comin'?"

The eyes of the arrogant will be humbled
and human pride brought low;
the LORD alone will be exalted in that day.

—Isaiah 2:11

Don't be humble…you're not that great.

—Golda Meir

*Friday, 4 November 2011, Late in the Evening, At the Bottom of*
*Quebrada Barranca Blanco (White Canyon Gorge), Northern Perú*
*(8° 08'20.32" S, 78° 42'37.60" W—Elevation 5,620')*

When I was a small boy, my father would often lie with me in the soft grass of our yard, and with my head cradled on his arm, we would pick out images in the soft white clouds floating above. "There's Charlie Brown," he'd say, pointing up at some slowly churning white mass in the sky.

"And Linus!" I'd add. I could conjure up just about any image my imagination desired. It was great fun, a very special memory.

I was very close to my father. He died in 2008, just six months after we lost my brother Glenn. That sad spring I was at Dad's side to the end, administering morphine under his tongue as needed—just the two of us in his Nebraska living room.

Now here I lay, also dying, in a remote canyon in the central Andes. But I was alone. I would die alone. *Why?*

- - - - -

When I next woke, it was very dark. Night had fallen, and it was late. At first I had no idea where I was. Looking around, I was suddenly saddened to see that I was still in that deep quebrada. I had no idea how long I had been asleep. Looking up into the sky framed by the canyon's walls, I was treated to a majestic view of beautiful clouds illuminated by a full moon. They were floating by and reminded me of those long-forgotten happy times with Dad during my childhood.

I then began to see images in the clouds. Unlike the vague, ill-defined shapes of my youth, these images were surprisingly sharp and looked remarkably like black-and-white photos. The first to appear, of all things, was our favorite Yorkshire terrier, Shadow. I smiled at his image leaping happily in the sky like Superman. Then other images appeared. I could make out the face of a woman named Julia. She was my brother-in-law José's mother, who had died a few years earlier. This puzzled me, because I had not known Julia all that well. In fact, I had met her only three or four times and could not understand why I would conjure up her image. *What's with this?* Julia sweetly smiled down at me. Her cloud drifted past and was replaced by the image of my father, a clear and distinct face in a fresh cloud. I missed my dad and was deeply saddened by that image. Dry tears cramped my eyes.

Next came the visage of my mother-in-law, Evelina, who had died in 2002 and was also dearly missed. She, too, sweetly smiled down at me. With even more emotion I began to cry again—dry, painful tears.

Waiting for the next image, I drifted back to sleep.

- - - - -

*Saturday, 5 November 2011, Early in the Predawn Morning, At the Bottom of Quebrada Barranca Blanco (White Canyon Gorge), Northern Perú*
*(8° 08'20.32" S, 78° 42'37.60" W—Elevation 5,620')*

Sometime later, during the darkest part of the night, I again was awakened, this time by the distinct sound of footsteps and shoes scraping on the rocks around me. I suffer from premature hearing loss and am nearly deaf, so I was surprised at how clearly I heard this. I had a visitor.

I opened my eyes and clearly saw my brother Glenn standing over me. He was clad in jeans and a flannel shirt, with elbows cocked, hands facing aft—so typical of him. He was framed by the canyon walls with the white clouds and full moon behind him. Pumping his left thumb in a come-along motion and gesturing toward the bamboo grove, he clearly said in his familiar voice, "Hey, Scott. You comin'?"

Then as quickly as he had appeared, he was gone. I heard and felt the gravel splaying off a nearby boulder as he sprinted off. I shot up and struggled to my feet, but I was too slow. He had already disappeared. My heart was palpitating wildly as I looked around, expecting Glenn to come bounding back. But I found myself alone and surrounded by the quiet cold of the deep desert canyon.

I spent the rest of the night trying to understand what had happened. It was all bizarre. First there were the faces in the clouds, clearly visible, and then the all-too-vivid visit from my dead brother. *What was the message?* Were people in heaven preparing to welcome me? And just to *where* did my brother want me to follow him? Did he want me to go back up the dry quebrada and into the green grove of reeds and thickets that he seemed to be pointing to?

I could no longer sleep, so I lay there and went over my options. There weren't many. *Come on, genius!* I scolded myself. *You're the problem solver, the troubleshooter. You're the first sergeant. The guy all those people— those airmen, officers, even commanders—came to for answers. You're the fixer upper. Well, fix this!*

As if I were chewing out some wayward airman and trying to get through to him, I shouted, "God gave you a brain. *Use it, dummy!*" Then, in less than a whisper, I said to myself, "Well, fool, what are you gonna do?"

## Brother Love

When you're young, four years is a long time. So my brother Glenn, four years older than I, seemed to be from another generation. But as childhood playmates, we were close. Then once Glenn reached puberty, his interests naturally became different from mine. But he never stopped reaching out to me and was always a good brother.

We moved to East San Jose in the early 1960s. At the time the area was full of farms and fruit orchards. One of Glenn's first girlfriends lived at the end of our street. Her name was Ginger, and she was half Japanese. Her dad, like ours, was in the navy. In the mid-1960s Ginger's dad was killed in an off-duty shooting incident in the Philippines. I remember Glenn spending a lot of time that summer at their house, doing chores and comforting Ginger and her mom. Ginger's mom spoke little English, and Glenn would often accompany her to the market and help her shop. That was Glenn at his best.

In the crazy spring of 1969, when madness and riots broke out in more than two hundred American cities, San Jose was not spared. By that time Glenn was in high school and hanging out with some pretty rough people.

Later that year, on a Saturday in December, fifteen-year-old Glenn sneaked away with some of his rough friends to the Altamont Speedway where the Woodstock of the West, as the news dubbed it—or "some free hippie concert," as my dad later called it—was taking place. Glenn just disappeared, and my folks were alternately frantic and livid. When he came home Sunday night, he was a mess. Glenn had obviously had a rough weekend.

Glenn caught hell from Mom and Dad, which resulted in one of the few instances of violence I ever witnessed from my dad. He and Glenn really got into it, and fists flew in the kitchen, and the fighting spilled into the family room. Glenn ended up slamming his fist into the solid fire door leading to the garage and broke his hand badly. That was Glenn at his worst.

After finishing high school Glenn joined the navy. Three years later I enlisted in the air force. Because our assignments kept us in different parts of the world, I rarely saw Glenn over the next three decades.

– – – – –

When I was stationed in Okinawa, Japan, and attached to a special operations unit, I often traveled to Cubi Point Naval Air Station in the Philippines to train with the Navy SEALs there. On one such trip I found that Glenn's ship, the USS *Saratoga,* was pulling into port. I went to the pier and was piped aboard and surprised him. He paid a shipmate to take his shore patrol duty that night, and we hit the town.

That's when I met his girlfriend, Lina. I stayed in their rented house and soon realized that Lina was special. She brought him all sorts of joy and was his anchor. I was able to visit them once or twice more over the next several months.

In May 1979 I applied for thirty days of leave and hopped a military flight back home to California. My visit was anything but pleasant. On my second or third day home, I got into an argument with Dad over my use of the family car. When it got heated, my mom stepped in and sided with my dad. I threw my gear in my duffel, walked out, and hitchhiked up to Fairfield, where I caught the next military flight to the Philippines. I spent the rest of my leave with Glenn and Lina.

They had been a couple for some time and were as good as married, but he couldn't get permission from his commander to tie the knot. I didn't know it at the time, but he had already written our folks and told them of his intention to marry Lina. It didn't sit well with them.

When I returned to Okinawa, I found a letter from my mom waiting for me, apologizing for her part in my "messed-up leave." Then she explained their reservations regarding Glenn's marrying a Filipino girl "when there are two races and cultures and religions involved." I realized that, in spite of my parents' opinions, I really wanted my brother to find happiness and wished the best for him.

In June I was back in the Philippines and again stayed at Glenn and Lina's place. Glenn told me that he was soon to ship out on an extended Indian Ocean cruise and had in fact already married Lina (albeit illegally in the eyes of the navy) in a local ceremony.

That summer, while Glenn was at sea, Lina secured a visa to visit her sister in Colorado. While there, she was killed in a car accident. As Glenn was at sea and not officially married, he was not notified of Lina's death for a couple of months. When he returned to Subic Bay, he learned the tragic news. I think that is what pushed him over the edge.

When I visited him a few months later, he was a complete mess. His drinking had gotten out of hand, and eventually the navy denied him reenlistment. After serving on three aircraft carriers and with most of his time at sea, he left the navy with far less than the twenty years needed for a pension.

From then on, Glenn lived a hard life, and he made some bad decisions. He moved from place to place, living for a while with our parents in California and later in Iowa. Then after several years of bouncing around the Pacific Northwest, Glenn withdrew into a sort of self-imposed exile to face his many demons. For a long time he lived like a hermit in the Oregon backwoods.

– – – – –

Over the years I tried to contact Glenn. Finally via letters and phone calls, we reconnected. I really wanted to see him, but something always came up. I suspected he was not yet ready to come back into the family fold, and I respected his wishes.

At last, in December 2006, I convinced him to come to Texas for a visit. He had been granted a long-delayed Veterans Administration claim, and for the first time in many years, he had some extra cash. He told me he had always wanted to take a long rail trip, and he boarded a train from Oregon that would take him through the Rocky Mountains en route to San Antonio.

Glenn called me late on a Friday afternoon and said he'd found the train unbearable. He was in Colorado and didn't want to continue. I told him to wait there. I drove through the night and picked him up in Denver the next day. From there we headed east, stopping to see our folks in Nebraska. Mom and Dad hadn't seen Glenn in many years, and it was a good visit. Then we headed off to Iowa to see other relatives. In Davis County, Iowa, where our dad grew up, we visited with Uncle Ron and Aunt Sue, two very special people. After that we took our time rolling south to my home in Texas.

My brother Glenn.

Glenn was able to renew his acquaintance with Carito and meet our three daughters. We shared a wonderful family Christmas together. He left on New Year's Eve to fly back to the West Coast.

Over the following months I talked to him frequently, and he told me several times how much he had enjoyed his visit and our time together.

Glenn died the following November at the age of fifty-three. During our holiday visit he must have known that he was sick, but he never let on. I will always have the memory of our time together that Christmas season, and I still thank the Lord for those three weeks.

I missed Glenn terribly after he was gone. Little did I know that I would see him again in the strangest of circumstances—and that he would help save his little brother's life.

## An Idea

I awoke again during this amazing and strange night and immediately knew that, in my present condition, there was no way I could climb out of that canyon. And I was convinced that life-giving water was nearby; I just had to find it and collect it. All those tall green cane stalks grew there because of a water source. I then thought back to my survival training. *Yeah,* I thought, *just maybe… Yes! That's it! A solar still! It just might be possible. It has to be possible! I can build a solar still.*

Almost all soil holds water. This quebrada definitely had evidence of moisture with that cane grove and particularly in the clay I had scooped out of the hole the day before.

In my survival training, we had learned how to construct a solar still. My plan was to dig one, possibly two, wide, shallow holes and place a piece of plastic formed into a cup at its lowest point. I then would cover the hole with a section of my poncho and secure the edges with stones. In the middle of the sheet, I would place a small stone to weigh it down. As the soil warmed and the water underground evaporated upward, it would re-form as droplets on the underside of the sheet, and then they would drift to the center of the sheet where the rock rested. The collected droplets would drip into the cup below, and *bingo!* Water!

To fuel the process, I would place the clay from the hole in the cane grove I had dug the day before at the bottom of my still. I knew all too well that the water I might collect would be foul. But at least some of the impurities would not evaporate with the moisture and be drawn up and onto the sheet. I eagerly awaited the coming dawn.

About 5:30 a.m. I got up. I still felt exhausted, and all my muscles and joints ached. I reached for my empty water bottle and knocked it, bouncing into a small dip. Bats above me darted about, making their way to their daytime roosts in the cliff sides.

About then a bout of diarrheic spasms doubled me over, and I was struck by the reality of my dire situation. I again referred to my world map. Libya was my next target, then parts of Egypt and Algeria came out with a disturbing tear diagonally deep into Mali. *Oh well.*

Since my descent off the edge of the puna, I had consumed only about two liters of water. In fact that's all the water I had drunk since dinner at José and Sheila's home two and a half days earlier. I was in deep kimchi.

I leaned against a rock and thought about last night's bizarre events, the faces in the clouds. Except for José's mother, Julia, whom I hardly knew, I had many fond and precious memories of them all. Even seeing Shadow had brought me a sense of joy.

Then there was Glenn's visit, along with his clear words and gestures. What was that all about? Glenn had pointed me back to the green grove where earlier I had used my underwear to squeeze bad water out of clay. I realized it was early Saturday morning, November 5. November 8 would mark the fourth anniversary of Glenn's death. I didn't know what to make of it except that, in my delirium, I might be losing my mind.

– – – –

Again I painfully worked my way back over the thorn-covered boulders and into the cane grove. There I crawled through the dry thicket and on my belly looked down into the hole I had dug the day before, still hoping that the small cistern was full of water that had seeped in overnight. Instead, I found an even drier hole. What had been slightly damp clay at the bottom was now caked and felt like dry sand. I was disappointed, bordering on despondent.

I dug deeper into the hole and eventually retrieved several handfuls of slightly moist clay, which I scooped into my Tilley hat and shirt. Then with no small effort I returned to my makeshift camp, crawling over the same path to the sandy riverbed.

Still energized by my plan and the hope it brought me, I selected a relatively level area of sand and gravel and began to dig. I used my knife to help chop through the worst parts of the packed, stony soil. It took a while to get the hole deep enough that my poncho would cover it properly. While I worked, sudden gusts of wind kicked up, and the newly dug-up soil would blow over the sheet. Trying to make repairs and clean off the tarp by kneeling at the sides of the hole, I unintentionally collapsed it several times. It was very frustrating, but after about an hour and a half, I had finished two primitive solar stills.

Despite my exertion, I realized I was not sweating. My body was bone dry. My skin was scaly and flaccid. When I pinched the flesh on my forearm, it stayed in the wrinkled form long after I let go—an obvious sign of advanced dehydration. *Not good,* I thought.

My thirst was terrible, and despite the raging diarrhea I knew would result, I returned to my pit in the grove and squeezed more droplets of precious moisture through my shorts and licked greedily at the foul, salty silt.

By the time I got back from the cane grove, the sun was making its appearance, and the temperature had risen significantly. I found that the wind had blown so much sand and dust over my newly constructed stills that the plastic had collapsed into the holes. I worked to clean them out and pack the damp clay along the sides and bottom. By the time I had the clay gathered from the hole in the cane grove in my stills, it was dried out and useless. I felt as though I was running in circles, and just as I was about to head back to the grove, I was again racked with cramps and more diarrhea.

Lying there doubled up in pain, I saw the wind blow the poncho material off the top of my water stills. Then the holes filled with more dust and sand.

"Oh, Lord! Help me!" I cried out loud in angst.

## 10

# The Miracle

Get wisdom, get understanding....
Though it cost all you have, get understanding.

—**Proverbs 4:5, 7**

*Saturday, 5 November 2011, Early Morning, At the Bottom of Quebrada Barranca Blanco (White Canyon Gorge), Northern Perú (8° 08'20.32" S, 78° 42'37.57" W—Elevation 5,620')*

Once things started to go bad for me, I repeatedly turned to God and asked him again and again for help. At first I asked, and then I begged him to spare me, rescue me, help me. But things continued to go from bad to worse.

I now know that all my prayers were for solely selfish reasons. They were things *I* wanted. It never occurred to me that I needed to follow the apostle John's guidance: "If we ask anything *according to his will,* he hears us. And if we know that he hears us—whatever we ask—we know that we have what we asked of him."[3]

"According to his will"—that was the key. So far I had been asking for what *I* wanted—specifically, to be rescued and brought back to a world of water and chilled beverages. Like so many people, I can be very self-sufficient, relying too much on my own abilities and too often ignoring God's plan for my life. Even the way I had approached this walk. I'd not asked God about it. I hadn't asked for his blessing or guidance. Fueled by my own desires and goals, I had attempted my simple eight-hour walk for my own ends and pleasure. Now I was facing the consequences.

Having failed in my efforts to apply my own skills and training to building a solar still, I found I was out of ideas.

I needed a miracle.

James wrote, "If any of you lacks wisdom, you should ask God, who gives generously to all without finding fault, and it will be given to you. But when you ask, you must believe and not doubt, because the one who doubts is like a wave of the sea, blown and tossed by the wind."[4]

After the amazing events of the night before, I sensed it was critical for me to return to that thatch grove and to the dry hole I had dug in the riverbed the day before. Seeking escape from the oppressive sun and heat, I struggled back to the green grove and the filtered shade it offered. Once there I collapsed next to my barren hole and was overcome with complete and painful sadness. I felt so guilty for what I had done. I could only think about how my arrogance had brought me to this point. Now those who loved and relied on me would be affected and unfairly let down by my disappearance.

That's what it would be, a disappearance rather than a death. I figured my body would never be found, so there would always be a lingering question about my fate. My wife and daughters would always hold out some hope that I would someday reappear. However, a gringo gone missing in South America is not that unusual. In Colombia, for instance, guerrillas have been known to kidnap Westerners and hold them captive, sometimes for years. My loved ones would wonder, *Was that his fate?* Silence would be their answer. How long would it be before someone suggested I might have wanted to disappear? And painful doubts might then set in.

This was so unfair to them! I had really messed up.

My thoughts turned to my three daughters—the last time I'd seen each of their pretty faces, heard their sweet voices, told them I loved them. All that came to my mind were regrets at not having spent more time with them, not doing more for them, not being a better father.

Then I recalled seeing Carito off at the Lima airport. What was it now—only six days ago? It seemed much longer than that. So much had happened. How I wished I had held her a little longer and kissed her once more.

"Lord, what more can I do? I don't know what else to do! I'm so sorry," I cried out.

Then I recalled the day before when I had felt similarly despondent and completely defeated. I thought of my prayer then and again fervently prayed. I whispered hoarsely, "Whatever you want, Lord. I accept your will. Your will is my will, Lord. Whatever you want."

It stung to breathe through my dry, cracked throat, and I hurt all over. I laid my head down and fell asleep.

## Water Where There Was None

I woke to a calm quiet in the midmorning shadows. I was at peace, and for a moment I felt no pain or discomfort. I wondered briefly, *Am I dead?* I just lay there and repeated my prayer of gratitude for being in this place of shade and comfort.

Then a strange, foreign sound caught my attention—*gluurp*. It was close but so odd. I craned my head and waited. Then slightly higher pitched, it came again. *Gluurp-chk.* At first I thought it might be a bird, but that didn't seem right. The sound was much too close. Perhaps it was a lizard. I looked around the thatch and dead brush that made up the bed of the grove. But there wasn't a living thing looking back at me. Then about three feet away and a foot above me, I spied a twinkle in the filtered sunlight. Drops of moisture. *Water?* Just the smallest bit of water there in the thatch, and to my amazement it seemed to be moving. It was ever so faintly...*burbling.* I stared, not believing my eyes. Slowly, pulsing up and into the cane thatch bed, a place that was bone dry an hour earlier, there it was! I watched it rise and pulse in tiny throbs as it came from...nowhere. *Water!*

*Was this a mirage?* I reached out to it and pressed my fingers into the

The green grove, where water miraculously appeared.

moist leafy bed. It was true! I felt cool liquid on my fingers. I was astounded! I expected it to be foul like the silt squeezed through my underwear, but as I brought my moistened fingers to my mouth, I was thrilled and ecstatic to taste sweet, sweet water. *Oh, Jesus! Oh, Jesus! Thank you! Thank you! Thank you!*

*This* was answered prayer.

I struggled to grab the empty water bottle from my sack, and I pressed a scrap of plastic down into the thatch like a crude cup. I then took a sip of the clear, cool water. I was so parched that it took several more sips before any of the liquid made it down my throat.

I was elated. I sang out loud, "Thank you, Jesus! Thank you, Jesus! For saving me!" Then I got busy filling my water bottle. I got it about half full and couldn't wait any longer. I tipped the bottle up to my cracked lips and drank deeply. The clear water, even with the debris and leafy matter from the floor of the cane patch mixed in, was *so* good.

Before long the bottle was empty, and I worked to fill it again. After another half hour or so, I got it about halfway full again and drank more, this time in deep, slow, wonderful sips. It tasted and felt so good to have water inside me once more. I feared the miracle brook would vanish as quickly as it had appeared, so I worked to fill my bottle completely.

It took some time to scoop the precious fluid with my cupped hand and dribble it into my two-and-a-half-liter bottle. While doing this, I began to believe that just maybe I was not doomed after all. It was simply amazing. I knew it was a miracle, clear and simple, and I had no doubt that the Lord alone had saved me.

I sang more praises.

Lying there in the shade of the cane grove, I was overwhelmed with emotion and gratitude. I knew I was a witness to a clear and obvious physical miracle. After all, this small spring emerged *above* the lowest point in the riverbed and appeared from what was, moments before, absolutely dry and barren soil. How could it be? It no longer was a question *if* God could make water appear where none was or even should be. I knew that he had.

Among our physical needs, water is at the top of our hierarchy of essentials for survival, and God has been in the water business for some time. Like the time the Israelites arrived at a place called Rephidim and found no water. The people became upset and dangerously restless. After unsuccessfully trying to reason with them, Moses turned to the Lord, and God instructed him to go on ahead with some of the elders. At a place called Horeb, he was to strike the rock with his staff "and water will come out of it for the people to drink."[5] He did, and the water flowed.

Before my ordeal if you had asked me if God could bring water to a place where there was none, I would have said something like, "Of course he can. I *believe* God can do anything he desires." But since my episode in the desert, I now bear witness that I *know* God can do such things.

## A New Hope

I felt so fresh, so new. I was invigorated and began to believe I might make it out of the canyon after all. Then as quickly as the spring had appeared, the water stopped flowing, and before long there was no more water to scoop up and collect. But I had managed to gather nearly five liters—half I had drunk immediately, and the other half I had stored in my bottle.

Now it was midday, and since I had a belly full of water and a full bottle, I wondered if I might be able to make it to Poroto before dark. If so, from there I could catch a bus or a combi back to Trujillo and be at José and Sheila's house that night. I was excited at the possibility!

I took out my map and compass and again tried to establish where I was. I believed I was on track near a place called Huayabito in Quebrada El Potrenillo (Potrenillo Gorge), so marked on my chart. If correct, I was a mere five miles from my destination!

I figured all I needed to do was climb out of the canyon and rejoin the trail. From there it looked like the going would get progressively easier as I descended into the Río Chepén valley and walked the final two-plus miles to Poroto.

Fueled with water and renewed confidence, I was thrilled at the prospect of finally getting out of these mountains. I gathered my things and prepared for the tough ascent.

# The Box Canyon

It always looks darkest just before it gets totally black.

—Charlie Brown

When one door is closed, don't you know, another is open.

—Bob Marley

*Saturday, 5 November 2011, 1200 Hours, Ascent from the Bottom of Quebrada Barranca Blanco (White Canyon Gorge), Northern Perú (8º 08'20.32" S, 78º 42'37.60" W—Elevation 5,620')*

Revived by the water, at first I felt more than able to climb out of the deep canyon. However, I soon realized I had underestimated my weak state. Before long I was sweating profusely and panting, only able to climb a few steps at a time. I stopped frequently to rest, so the going was very slow.

It took me more than two hours to make it back up to the trail I had left the day before. Once there I was able to see farther down the canyon, and in the dusky haze I struggled to get a compass reading on some distant landmark.

- - - - -

When I was only nine years old, I was an enthusiastic Boy Scout, eager to prove my prowess in surviving in the wild. In 1969 I needed to complete an exercise with a compass to earn a promotion to First Class Scout. This was why I was leading a column of fellow Scouts along a narrow trail near Coyote Reservoir, close to Gilroy, California. In my hand I clasped a 1964 Silva Ranger Type 15 deluxe compass with optional adjustable declination, clinometer, and quadrant scale.

At the time Sears, Roebuck and Company was the authorized distributor of all essential scout gear. My dad had bought this exceptional compass for me there, and I treasured it. We were not well off, and luxuries simply did not exist in our household. But Dad saw the usefulness and importance of this tool and purchased it for me. My dad was a naval aviator, and he made a point of schooling me on the use and utility of a map and compass. He'd often quiz me on the various map symbols and count on me to track our progress, location, and mileage on our frequent family road trips.

On the 1969 scouting exercise, I was proud to have what I believed to be the ultimate land navigational instrument and did my best to orient myself to it and to my map so I could make methodical and precise calculations. My brother Glenn, who was a Life Scout, was the senior patrol leader on the compass exercise and diligently waded through the tall, dry, brown weeds off to my left, but he looked bored. I needed to excel on this exercise to complete the requirements for the higher rank. I wanted it badly, but I knew Glenn wouldn't cut me any slack.

I checked my map and then my compass once again. I knew I was right on the mark. I led the patrol off the trail and down into an oak-shrouded hollow. The burrs and stickers clung to our socks and trousers, but I urged the others on. "Not far now," I said. Then reaching the shady ravine, I took another bearing and, looking south, spied my goal: a neat pile of three stones atop each other. Victory! I had located the way point!

My patrol mates slapped me on the back and passed official BSA canteens around for a needed gulp of water. I took particular pride in having Glenn sign me off on this task.

Since that day I have always had a high comfort level with using a compass.

– – – – –

At my present location in the Andes, all the mountains and ridges looked alike. More worrisome was that both of my compasses seemed to be performing strangely. The bearing from one compass indicated that the canyon below ran northeast to southwest, but according to my map the canyon ran southeast to the northwest—completely opposite. The other compass indicated a similar reading but was a few degrees different. Why did the compass information conflict with my map?

Then I remembered an adage I'd often heard in the air force: there are old aviators, and there are bold aviators, but there are no old, bold aviators. Pilots are trained to trust their instruments. When their physical senses tell them one thing and their aircraft instruments tell them another, they are taught to ignore their senses and trust their instruments. For example, while flying in a cloudy sky, a flyer might *feel* he is flying straight and level, but his instruments might indicate he is actually in a dive or a turn. Aviators must ignore their sensory data and follow their gauges.

I am not a pilot, but I served on an aircrew for eight years and often heard this maxim. My compass was telling me one thing while my chart and my gut instinct were telling me another. I chose to trust my instruments, my compasses.

Looking at my map and believing I was near the obscure place labeled as Huayabito in Quebrada El Potrenillo (Potrenillo Gorge), I was confident I was only about four and a half miles from Poroto. On the map I saw the elevation lines were comfortably and gradually spaced farther and farther apart, indicating a gradual descent.

*Easy going ahead,* I concluded with some comfort.

Looking down the canyon in the direction of my planned route, I also saw I would be following a trail along three gradually descending, extended saddleback ridges. *Easy!* I was eager to get going, optimistic, and thankful, knowing the Lord had spared me in that canyon with the gift of water when all reason said there should be none. I couldn't wait to tell people about the miracle I had witnessed. I took a deep swallow from my water bottle and was off. The container was already nearly one-third empty, but I was confident I'd be in Poroto before I ran out of water again.

I took another compass bearing and turned right to cross a series of low, smooth, rocky bluffs, convinced I'd join Río Chepén at any time. The route was easy, and while the path was faint and hard to discern at times, thankfully it was clear of most of the thorny brush and cacti I had contended with the previous two days. As I trudged along, I sang praises and would have whistled if I'd had enough spit to do so.

## Hopes Dashed

Constantly exposed to the sun on the open ridgeline, I sweated profusely. Before long my legs burned anew from the exertion of the constant descent. I was hot and often returned to my dwindling supply of God-given sweet water for refreshment.

I was making great time and covered what felt like a couple of miles pretty quickly. I anticipated dropping at any time into the Río Chepén valley but saw only more low mountains ahead. At least the trail was descending, and the going was not all that hard.

After a couple of hours, though, I felt some anxiety. Why was it taking so long to reach the Río Chepén? Surely by now I'd covered at least the four or five miles to the dry riverbed. In fact, I knew I must have covered at least twice that distance. I took another compass reading that told me now I was heading southwest. That couldn't be right! My chart clearly showed that the path I believed I was on should be running northwest. *What is wrong? Is my compass damaged? Could both of them be messed up?* I was utterly confused.

My Boy Scout and air force survival training were of little help here. I couldn't look for moss on the north side of trees. In this barren wasteland there were no trees. I did however note that the early-afternoon sun was now beating down on the right side of my face, indicating that I was heading more south than north. A twinge of worry shot through my body. I took another drink and noted my water bottle was less than half-full. I moved up to a nearby rise to get a better view of the canyon ahead and to my joy saw far ahead and below a wide, dry riverbed. I was confident this was Río Chepén. I was almost there! "Thank you, Jesus!" I said out loud, over and over.

I put out of my mind the confusion of my compass bearings.

As I neared the wide riverbed, I noticed how dramatically the landscape had changed. I was no longer in the high mountains framed by dramatic canyons in all directions. Now I saw before me a shallow and wide, boulder-strewn riverbed carpeted with various cacti, debris, and bushes. The riverbed looked to be more than a half mile wide. I took another compass reading, and now it indicated that this dry river ran northward—exactly what my chart indicated and the direction I needed to go. I was overjoyed and started walking north.

It was midafternoon, and as I made my way down into the riverbed, I remained confident that I'd be sleeping in a bed that night. I yearned to make the last miles into Poroto as quickly as possible but now faced new obstacles. There were huge piles of ancient debris and waves of ten-foot-high piles of gravel and rocks in the riverbed, all indicating infrequent but violent flooding. It was obvious, too, that water had not visited this place in quite a while: the soil was bone dry, yet countless thorny plants and cacti thrived here.

There was no longer a trail or any donkey droppings, which I had come to regard as road signs that I was on a path. I was forced to weave and dance between the piles of sand, boulders, and foreboding cactus sentinels. Worse were the small camouflaged clusters of long spiny surprises on the ground, which I regarded as land mines. Every time I became complacent and stepped on one, I was rewarded with dozens of burning, stinging spines impaled in my foot or ankle. These barbed hazards slowed me down considerably.

With nearly every step I encountered cacti and other spiny surprises.

The afternoon sun was unrelenting, and I noted that I had just one-quarter of my water left. It seemed I had been on this riverbed for days. I trudged on and on, ever northward along the tough, uneven ground. In that low place it was hard to judge my progress because it lacked any good distant view. Hour after hour I walked, feeling as if I were on a treadmill, walking trance-like in place with the rough landscape rolling beneath me on a conveyor belt.

Then, dazed, I would step into another minefield of cacti or step on a loose stone. Or I'd encounter a pile of debris too large to climb over and have to deviate or, worse, backtrack on my path. I was usually walking forward but always weaving left and right, up and down. Gauging distance traveled in this landscape was simply impossible.

It was the roughest, most difficult-to-navigate terrain I had ever seen. My inexpensive, low-top walking shoes were nearly shredded and loaded with piercing burrs and thorns. I also worried about twisting an ankle or breaking a leg. Either would be the end!

At one point, as I clambered over a tall pile of debris, I could see for some distance. I took another compass reading and was alarmed that it indicated the riverbed was heading northeast rather than slightly north-west, as it should have been. I also noted that the steep, dry hills on both sides of the riverbed were now closer together. The riverbed seemed to be narrowing—and climbing? This wasn't right! Río Chepén should be de-scending and spreading out into a much wider and fertile green plain as it approached Poroto and joined the always wet Río Moche. Perhaps the tightening of the river course was an optical illusion. I continued on.

In spite of the much-appreciated gift of water, I now felt very weak. I thought of Flor's liver dinner three days ago at José and Sheila's home in Trujillo. It had been my last meal, and at the time I choked it down, not wanting to hurt Flor's feelings. At this moment I'd have settled for liver every day for the rest of my life to get out of this place! Just thinking of that meal brought severe hunger pangs—the first I recalled having.

With the massive calories I had been expending, it was no wonder I was famished. I stopped to rest and suddenly wanted desperately to lie down and sleep. I was so weary but feared that if I lay down now, it might be nearly impossible to get up again.

*God, forgive me for what I have done to my family,* I prayed.

Sitting there in the sun, I contemplated my situation. I seriously con-sidered backtracking all the way to the puna where I'd started. I knew there was water, the temperature was cooler, and there were people who could help me. But I realized I would never make it. I took another small sip of water and prayed, *Oh, Jesus, guide me. Give me strength and wisdom to follow your will.* With that I set off again.

About an hour later, now late afternoon, I stopped and again was overwhelmed with the desire to lie down and sleep. Instead, I looked around and was shocked to see that what had been a wide river valley was now a narrowing canyon. From where I was, I couldn't see far ahead but feared I had somehow wandered into a side arroyo. I crawled up a nearby mound of gravel and saw to my utter horror that I was in a box canyon. This obviously was not Río Chepén! I was totally devastated by the real-ization I was utterly, totally lost in this unforgiving place.

I desperately needed some relief. I looked around but saw only more of the same: dry, barren brush and sporadic gray-green columnar cacti watching over me like lonely sentinels. I wondered what these stately cacti might offer in the way of survival resources. I approached the nearest and surveyed its scarred and leathery surface.

With my pocketknife I sawed into the cactus and extracted a large, slightly moist wedge. I could not tell one species from another, but I knew that the fast-growing, mescaline-rich, and highly hallucinogenic plant known as the San Pedro cactus had been widely used in this region for thousands of years by the indigenous peoples—specifically by the local Moche tribes—for healing and religious practices. I also knew that taken improperly the San Pedro cactus could be lethal. I knew nothing about the other cacti in the area.

Not wanting to poison myself, I reluctantly threw away the moist slab of desert plant and pressed on.

## Boxed In

*Sat., 5 Nov., 1740 hours. Disappointment.*

*I now realize that what I thought was Río Chepén leading to Poroto is probably not. Still I'm baffled. I'm heading north up a major river canyon. According to my map & compass, this can only mean I'm headed to Río Moche. BUT, this riverbed is getting smaller, & now I see it's going uphill. ALL WRONG! The mtn due north looks like Mt. Poroto but is too far to reach today. I hate that Carito, Sheila & José will be worried. God willing I can reach civilization by tomorrow a.m.*

*I've seen no people since Thursday noon. No food since Wed. & water over half gone. I'm really in bad shape. What a dummy I am!*

– – – –

The realization that I was in serious trouble hung over me like a foreboding cloud. Maybe the decision was innocent, but I knew I'd made a bad call in following this river to a dead end. As I stood there, I noticed a persistent twitching in my thighs, and at the same time my skin itched all over. I also noticed I had stopped sweating some time ago. What did these symptoms mean? Was I having an allergic reaction to the countless cactus spines that had scratched me?

My bizarre compass was still telling me that I was in a riverbed running northeast to southwest. However, according to my map, there was no such river running in that direction anywhere near where I believed I was. I checked and rechecked the map. I was distraught, hot, and dehydrated and felt lightheaded and weak. I had only a single good sip of water left and was beginning to suffer from severe stomach cramps again, which I hoped were simply due to hunger. I wanted to believe that the five liters of water I had consumed today would keep me going for some time, but more likely that water had merely served to partially rehydrate my body from fluids previously lost. Whatever was left over I'd already sweated out.

Things looked bad. I knew this box canyon might literally be the end of the road for me.

I now realized I was no longer *of* the world or *in* the world. Instead, I was *out* of the world. I was in every sense apart from anything familiar and indeed was lost and adrift in the wilderness. For too long I had been completely separated from anything familiar, isolated from humanity, feeling completely and utterly alienated.

The realization that for so many hours I had drawn absolutely nothing from other people or from society was strangely sobering. Except for what I carried, which was very little, I saw or experienced virtually nothing that connected me to the world I'd left behind. There was of course the small abandoned choza that I had come across on my first day, but that might as well have been an ancient ruin from some long-failed civilization.

The term *no man's land* took on a whole new meaning. I used no electricity, ate no food, turned no taps to draw water, flushed not a single toilet, flipped no switches, pressed no buttons, spent no money, used no carbon-emitting machinery. Nor did I now demand a single human being's attention: physical, emotional, or otherwise.

I was on my own.

But I wasn't alone. My Lord Jesus Christ was at my side the whole time.

## An Unintentional Suicide Attempt

I found a level place near the western wall of the canyon that I hoped would provide some shade. I dropped my pack and pondered my precarious situation. About twenty feet from me there was a small anthill, and I went over to investigate. Scampering about were hundreds of large black ants, all going about their business. I wondered what they ate and, more important, what they drank. Then I became curious as to just how much protein was in an ant and how much moisture.

I had once lived in Panama, where we heard stories of the snakes, poisonous plants, and big cats of the jungle. However, after living there for four years, I realized that the true king of the jungle was in fact the ant. With the ants' unique survival skills, defense mechanisms, and sheer numbers, no creature could rival them in their ability to flourish in any environment.

Starving and thirsty, I impulsively picked up one of the larger ants and pinched it between my fingers. It crunched into a wet glob that I quickly flicked onto my tongue.

*Napalm!* That's the only word that comes to mind. The fire and coals that ignited in my mouth were indescribable. I gagged and choked, staggering, trying to spit out the inferno, but there was no relief. I scraped my tongue with a stick but continued to choke. My mouth filled with some foreign thing swelling and threatening to block my ability to breathe. Then the foreign thing began to emerge from my mouth. At first I thought it was a baby's foot, but then, to my horror, I realized it was my horribly swollen tongue. I rubbed sand on it, hoping to grind away some of the offending poison, but I was still choking—and it was getting worse. I fell back and tried not to panic, forcing myself to breathe slowly through my nose.

I lay there for some time wheezing and gagging, simply trying to stay alive. Gray shadows now engulfed the canyon as dusk descended. I don't know how long I waited for the effects of the ant poison to subside; I simply concentrated on breathing and staying calm. Just as the last bits of light faded, I sensed a presence to my left and slowly rolled my head to see who or what was there.

I had a visitor.

About three feet away was a rather large snake. But not just any snake. This was a wide-jawed, flat-headed viper with a head about the size of my fist. I shuddered—I hate snakes!

I froze and fought not to hyperventilate through my nose. Both our tongues were extended—his flicking, mine swollen and protruding. The black-eyed viper studied me, moving his slightly elevated head right and left. He repeatedly flicked his tongue, cocking his wide-jawed head ever so slightly, as if he were sizing me up and considering his next move.

I wondered if my swollen and extended tongue might be perceived as a threat to him. I hoped not, because there was no way I could get my tongue back in my mouth. I was terrified and afraid to even blink. I knew that a venomous bite would kill me. The creature then slowly moved, crawling out of my sight, around behind me, somewhere above my head. My thoughts ran wild. I briefly imagined him slithering down my shirt collar, so I involuntarily hunched my shoulders. Then ever so slowly I rolled my head to the right and saw to my horror that he was there, even closer to me than before, tongue flicking, head slowly swaying back and forth! I closed my eyes and waited for the inevitable strike. I envisioned his fangs sinking deeply into my neck, pumping deadly venom into me. I prayed that the end would be quick.

The expected strike didn't come. After a few minutes I worked up enough courage to open my eyes and saw that my visitor was gone. I almost passed out at that point and realized I had been holding my breath. *Thank you, Lord! Thank you,* I prayed silently.

I later reasoned that maybe the snake was simply curious and, perhaps sensing that I might be dead, had approached hoping to make a meal out of a smaller scavenger feeding on me. I was simply too big to eat and posed no threat to him.

Did I mention that I hate snakes?

Worse than liver.

- - - - -

As darkness descended, I sensed my tongue returning to its normal size. The burning was reduced to a mild inferno, and I thought I might actually survive my unintentional suicide attempt. I was actually surprised I was still alive. Between the ant poisoning and the snake, I felt myself lucky to still be breathing. And I knew it was in no way due to my own talents, training, or skills. I was still alive because God wanted me to be alive, and I was humbled and grateful.

But why? As I lay there looking up at the stars, I wondered why God had spared me. I felt so isolated and removed from all I had known before. I had not seen a trace of another human being in days—not a distant cloud of dust from a passing car, not a telltale power pole or wire, not even a jet contrail in the sky. I had not even seen a single piece of litter on the ground, not a footprint, nothing. I felt utterly alone. Then the most disturbing thought came to my mind. *What if I have already died? If so, how would I know?*

I remembered a time several years before when Carito and I had led a youth group from the air-base chapel to a work camp in Loving, New

Mexico. Some evenings after dinner we would all gather in a parking lot, lie down on the blacktop, and look up at the sky. In that isolated corner of the Southwest, it was easy to see the heavens lit up with a panorama of brilliant stars. The first time we did this, someone spotted a tiny light streaming across the sky above. It went from horizon to horizon, and we agreed it must be a satellite. Before long another, then another passed overhead. It became a contest to see who could first spot the next one.

*That's it*, I thought. *I'll spy a passing satellite—that uniquely man-made vehicle streaming across the heavens far overhead—and it will be evidence that I am still alive, still part of the human world.*

So I lay there and strained my eyes, studying the heavens above. Minutes passed. Then a half hour passed. An hour. Nothing. Just stars.

"Oh, God," I moaned, "this *can't* be heaven!" I was filled with sorrow, confusion, and fear.

I lay there for what seemed hours and watched as thin clouds high above slowly drifted by. I was at my lowest point. I seriously wondered if I was still alive or perhaps stuck in some etheric never-never land.

They say it is darkest just before dawn, but that isn't really true. In reality the darkest point of any evening is in the middle of the night—equally distant from dusk and dawn. Lying there in the funeral-dark dirt, I finally drifted off to sleep.

# Day 4

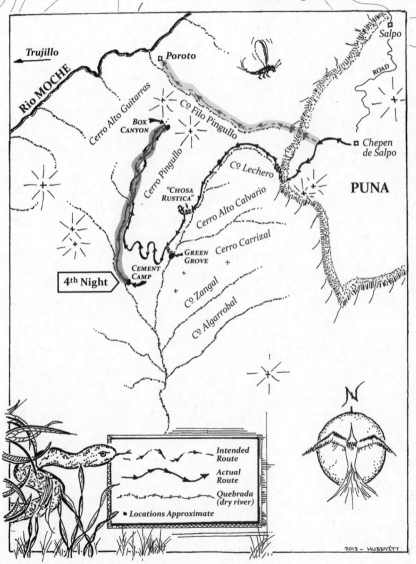

# 12

# The Road

When it is darkest, men see the stars.

—Ralph Waldo Emerson

Life's funny like that.

—Floyd Rayburn

*Sunday, 6 November 2011, Dawn, Quebrada El Peñón
(8° 07'25.95" S, 78° 46'37.31 W—Elevation 3,258')*

*Sun., 6 Nov., 635 hours*

*Cold last night. On my way at 5:30 a.m. before sunup. Realize
this canyon is dead end—heading back down to what I pray is
Río Chepén. Will sleep when it's hot to save water. Only ¼ bottle
left. Urine too bad to drink anymore.*

*I love you, niñas… I love you, Carito. I want to see you
again. Lord, hear my prayer.*

– – – – –

Throughout the night the Lord and I got pretty close. It wasn't just because he was the only one to talk to. He was the *best* one to turn to. It
occurred to me late that night just how blessed I was to have all this time
to focus only on him, to not be distracted by *anything*. Absolute focus.
Sort of like buddy time or maybe guys' night out. Better yet, it was qual-
ity Father and son time.

Proverbs calls us to "Get wisdom, get understanding.... Do not forsake wisdom, and she will protect you; love her, and she will watch over you."[6]

While I didn't recall those wise words at the time, that message was being received loud and clear in my heart. I yearned for understanding. If I had died, as I had fully expected to do several times during this ordeal, I knew I would have reaped the consequences for my foolish pursuits. But I hadn't been asked to ante up my life—not yet at least.

The Lord was there for me and came through for me. He saved my life by causing water to spring up from the desert floor where there was none. He allowed me to survive the ant poison and protected me from the viper. He had spared me for a reason, and I was beginning to understand that I would not, could not perish until he was ready. He had plans for me.

I just needed to stay close to him, trust him, and somehow it would all be okay. If I did perish, I would simply be fulfilling his plan. I was no longer in control. *He* was.

Regardless of what God's plan was, I was still totally, hopelessly lost and again out of water. My compasses made no sense. Rescuers were not searching these canyons. Helicopters would not appear at any moment. Nobody was looking for me. And even if others had known where I intended to walk, I was clearly not on the correct track between Chepén and Poroto.

No one was coming for me.

Just for kicks I took another compass bearing and found that the riverbed had shifted thirty degrees since last night! Again I studied my chart and tried to guess where I had gone wrong. I really had no clue, but I knew that I needed to keep moving. To sit still was to die.

I was at the end of a box canyon, so going forward was futile. As much as I dreaded backtracking, I had no other choice. I looked down that riverbed, gathered my pack, slung it onto my sore back, and set off on what felt like a perpetual walk.

Overnight my swollen tongue had returned to its normal size—more or less. I had no sensation on it, and without saliva I couldn't tell if I could taste anything. I wanted to rinse out my mouth, but lacking water, I could only pick out the sand and gravel from my futile attempt to erase the searing pain of the ant poison. At least I was still breathing; I was walking and heading in the only direction left to me—things could be worse.

As I set off, I offered a prayer of thanks and said to the Lord, *Guide me and protect me to allow me to do your will.*

The sun rose, and the temperature climbed quickly. I noticed that everything around me looked different. Something was very wrong. This did not seem like the same canyon I had come up the afternoon before. The riverbed was not nearly as difficult to negotiate. And most strange, the dry riverbed was not spreading out into the wide, low, dry alluvial wash I had struggled through the day before. In fact, the ground was much more level and less cluttered with boulders, cacti, and debris. How could this be? Was this another miracle? I could not figure it out. There was no other route, no other canyon to retreat through. I had to be heading back through the canyon I had walked up yesterday. But it was not the same. I gave up trying to understand it and simply kept repeating, "Whatever you want, Lord. Whatever you want."

## No Explanation

By about 8:30 a.m. I hadn't progressed far when ahead of me, in the low hills to the right of the shallow riverbed, I saw something very strange. I stopped, squinted, and stared. I wasn't sure what I was seeing. I walked on. Perhaps it was an odd ridgeline or even a weird rock formation. But as I got closer, I realized it could be only one thing. It was a road. *A road!*

It was a dirt road winding down the side of the mountain and into the riverbed ahead of me. Clear as day, there it was. *How could I have missed it yesterday?* I was baffled. Then I knew I hadn't missed it. *It wasn't there yesterday. It simply was not there.* Or I wasn't in this streambed yesterday, but that simply was not possible. There was only one riverbed and one canyon. That road was too prominent for me to have missed it. Either in my delirium I had staggered past this obvious road the afternoon before, or perhaps I had stumbled upon the dry Río Chepén above the point where this road descended and joined it. However, it didn't matter! God had somehow put the road there for me to find.

*I found a road! I found a road!* was all I could think. *Thank you, Jesus!* A road meant people. And people meant rescue. I was elated! As I approached the place where the roughly graded dirt road ended its descent down the steep mountainside and joined the dry river valley, I shouted again and again, "Hallelujah! Thank you, Lord! Hallelujah!"

I stepped over the pile of dirt a bulldozer had left alongside the track in the soft sand and looked at the man-made road. Then I looked at the soft sandy soil beneath my feet, and the sight made me weep. There were scores of tire tracks and, better yet, footprints. Human footprints! I was beside myself with joy. *People were here. People come here. They walk and they drive here. Oh, thank you, sweet Jesus!*

Other than the ancient choza I'd come across on my second day, I had not seen a trace of another human. Being that alone takes a terrible toll on your spirits.

— — — — —

In January 1991 just before the outbreak of the first Persian Gulf War, I and nineteen other servicemen were tasked with ferrying twenty brand-new Jeep Cherokees, donated by the Kuwaiti government, to a remote army outpost along the Saudi-Iraqi border. Our destination was east of the plains of Ad Dibdibah and on the northern edge of the great Nefud Desert in what many would call the middle of nowhere. My vehicle was last in the convoy, and late in the afternoon it broke down, forcing me to pull over and watch the nineteen Cherokees ahead of me press on and disappear beyond the horizon. I was stranded along that frontier road with no radio or ability to call for help. No one had cell phones at the time, and even if I'd had one, I doubt there would have been any service.

After I had spent more than four hours without being able to flag down another vehicle for assistance, the already sporadic traffic diminished significantly. Darkness fell, and I started to worry. I felt as if I had fallen off the edge of the earth.

Sitting in the sand next to the beached Jeep, I cracked open a liter bottle of desalinated water and tried to enjoy the panoply of stars above me. It was magnificent. But being stranded in the desert of a looming war zone, away from anything familiar, was still unsettling. I felt completely separated from civilization. It was the most remote place I had ever been.

That is, until I got lost in the Andean desert.

— — — — —

Standing in that isolated Peruvian riverbed, staring down at the vehicle and human tracks in the dirt at my feet, I had trouble grasping that I was reconnecting with the human race. I kept repeating to myself, "People were here. People come here. They walk and drive here. Oh, thank you, sweet Jesus!"

In my condition I knew that climbing the road up the steep hill alongside the riverbed would be hard, so I reasoned that following the road down the riverbed gave me an equal chance of finding help and rescue. So I walked along the graded road, occasionally stepping in one of the scores of footprints as if that could put me in contact with my fellowman. High in the perfectly blue sky above, the sun beat down on me, but I no longer felt that I was being beaten down. I was filled with renewed hope. With more purpose in my steps, I followed the sandy and dusty road along the riverbed for about fifteen minutes. I had covered less than two-thirds of a mile when the road took a sudden left turn and abruptly ended. There, before me, were two neatly stacked piles of bagged cement. I stood there bewildered, my head cocked, trying to process this strange sight.

Not far away from the pile of cement bags, I saw another strange item, something I recognized from my past. It was a Stokes litter, a metal wire basket designed to rescue injured personnel by helicopter or on a wire-and-pulley transfer system between ships at sea. I had worked with these in the Air Rescue Service many decades before. What in the world was a Stokes litter doing in an isolated riverbed at the end of a dirt road in a Peruvian desert canyon? Was I seeing things?

I staggered over to investigate further and found a half-dozen brand-new shovels and a couple of iron pikes stacked neatly inside the ancient litter. No Peruvian in his right mind would leave such valuable tools unguarded. I anxiously craned my neck, scanning the surrounding hills for the owner of the tools. I called out but was able to emit only a hoarse croak. *Who owns these tools and cement?* I asked myself. None of it made sense. I sat down in the dirt next to the litter and tried to sort it all out.

*I must be hallucinating,* I concluded.

# 13

# Final Options

Men go abroad to wonder at the heights of mountains,
at the huge waves of the sea, at the long courses of the
rivers, at the vast compass of the ocean, at the circular
motions of the stars, and they pass by themselves without wondering.

—Augustine

*Sunday afternoon, 6 November 2011, Quebrada El Peñón
(Craggy Rock Gorge)
(8° 10'10.88" S, 78° 48'01.34" W—Elevation 2,253')*

After sitting in the hot midday sun for a long spell, I came up with a
theory. I deduced that men must have been mining cement here.
They had obviously found a suitable deposit here in the dry riverbed and
were harvesting and bagging it for later collection. Even if that were true,
the Stokes litter filled with tools confused me. The litter was an old ver-
sion, complete with wooden slats where the patient's back would have
been supported. It was probably vintage World War II gear. *How did it
get here?*

Whoever these workers were, they surely would return in the morning to resume their work. It was Sunday and probably their day off. All I
had to do was hang on until the next day. Tomorrow morning workers
would come and I would be saved! I tipped my bottle to my lips and
tapped its hollow end, but the last drops were long gone.

I knew that God had brought me to this place for a reason. He had plans for me. And I wondered if rescue was really only a nightfall away. I just had to make it until tomorrow morning. *Men will come,* I reassured myself.

I looked around for a suitable place to escape the scorching sun. It was only afternoon, and I had a wait of many hours ahead of me. About fifty feet away I spied a high bank with a clump of dead bushes along its top. I took four shovels from the litter, dragged them over to the bushes, pushed the shovels into the soft sand, and strung my towel between them. I then used what was left of my world map to cover the most sun-exposed side, securing the unfolded chart with small tabs of duct tape. It was a crude shelter but would provide some measure of protection through the afternoon heat. I slid underneath and, using my pack as a sort of pillow, settled in.

I said another prayer, thanking the Lord for this place, this road, and the people I hoped would arrive in the morning. I also asked him for wisdom and strength.

On day four while pondering my final choices at the cement camp, I took this photo of myself—a memory for my family if I died and my camera was found later.

## Taking Stock

Lying there I had ample opportunity to think about the past four days. I considered my situation and condition and was optimistic at the thought of men arriving in the morning to resume the work of the cement camp. They would surely have water and a method to get out of these mountains. Under my crude tent I was relentlessly tormented by swarms of flies and gnats. *Where do they get their water?* I wondered. *There must be a source nearby.* I looked at the brand-new shovels holding up my towel and appreciated the sliver of shade I was able to squeeze beneath. Before long I slipped into exhausted sleep.

Acute dehydration is a nasty business, and I knew I was severely dehydrated. I had all the symptoms: headache, dizziness, flushing, fatigue, disorientation, dry skin, poor judgment, lethargy, and on and on. From my survival training twenty-six years before, I knew my body held about fifty liters of fluid, and I realized that the symptoms of dehydration would become noticeable after the loss of as little as 2 percent, or one liter of water. At 5 to 6 percent water loss, two to three liters, I would experience grogginess, sleepiness, a headache, and tingling in the limbs. At 10 to 15 percent, five to seven liters, my skin would wrinkle and shrivel, my muscles might twitch uncontrollably, and delirium was probable. A loss above 15 percent would be fatal. So far I had experienced each of these symptoms to some degree, all except death.

The heat was unrelenting, and as the afternoon progressed and the sun swung around the sky toward the west, I had to shift my position to stay under the sliver of shade beneath my towel. My shoes were completely shredded, and I thought some fresh air would be beneficial to my feet. So I removed the pathetic shoes and peeled away my filthy socks. It was the first time they had been off since early Thursday morning, four days before.

What I saw added to my concern. My feet were in an appalling condition—raw, peeling, and battered. But where the skin was gone, I saw shiny, dry, red-gray craters. There were no leaking blisters. My feet were dry, shriveled, chewed up. Almost instantly the pesky insects surrounding me found my feet fascinating and made them their home base. I did my best to swat them away, but this was futile.

After lying there for a while, I was visited once more by a pair and then dozens of colorful, darting, energetic hummingbirds. They curiously hovered around the bank of dirt in front of me, where some small dusky-purple flowers especially interested them. I took great joy in watching them dart and hover about. They were not as vibrant as the Hillstars that had visited me high up near the puna. But these brown, green, and yellow birds were still beautiful. It was good to know something thrived in such a forlorn place.

Curious green lizards patiently perched on nearby rocks, motionlessly waiting for their next meal. I'm sure they were thankful I drew so many insects to their hunting grounds. I counted eleven around me at one time. A small one even crept up to my still foot and perched there for some time, looking for a meal. I tried not to think of the snake from the night before. Lizards are cool; snakes are not!

I wondered again about the men who worked in this riverbed and was amazed they would build a road through such extremely rough country just to mine cement. A road like that couldn't be cheap to build. How much profit could there be in cement? This thought perplexed and then haunted me. Next I thought of the shovels. They still had bright paint on their blades and had never been used. Suddenly I had a horrible thought: *What if those bags of neatly stacked cement weren't filled here? Maybe this isn't a cement mining camp. What else could it be?* I had no new ideas. I liked my first theory best: men would come in the morning.

But now I had a doubt. I began to worry what would happen if no one came to my rescue in the morning. I wasn't confident I would still be alive by then, so I started thinking again about the possibilities of walking out. After all there was a road leading up the mountain. It went somewhere; all I had to do was follow it.

I calculated there were at least three things wrong with my reasoning. First, in this heat and sun, I'd never make it. Second, in my condition I'd never make it. Third, the mountain was simply too steep. I'd never make it.

The time allowed me to sort through my knapsack and get organized. In doing so I made a wonderful discovery: squirreled away in a pocket of my bag was a spare set of thin reading glasses. I was thrilled at the find. I no longer needed to squint through the small magnifying glass to read my map! Using the glasses, I tried to locate my position, but even though I could once again clearly see my map, I still had no good idea where I was.

With so much time on my hands, I prayed and thought and then prayed some more. I thanked God for seeing me this far and over and over asked for his guidance and wisdom. In the course of the afternoon, I concluded I had only two options: I could lie here and wait for the men to rescue me, or I could lie here, and the men would never come, which would mean I would die waiting.

Thinking about these choices, I wondered if I really had any options. Perhaps things were going to follow the natural course of events. Maybe I wouldn't be rescued before I died. I was amused at this line of thinking, then irritated at my silly confusion. I giggled and wept at the same time.

Then I realized I actually had three options. I could lie here and wait for the men to rescue me. I could lie here, and the men would never come, and I would die here. Or I could wait for evening to come and walk out on that road.

After more thought, weighing the pros and cons, I decided the third option seemed best. I would be using the body and mind God had blessed me with. I concluded, *There is a road, and it goes somewhere, and it's cooler at night.* A plan began to develop.

The road would provide an easy path to follow, even at night. If I traveled light and only took what was essential, I believed I could cover ten to fifteen miles. Who knows, there might be a village right over that *first* hill. I'd rest until dusk and then make my final push up that road, up that mountain and, God willing, find help.

I reasoned, *if* men were coming along that road in the morning, I'd be that much closer to them and would be found sooner. By attempting to walk out, at least I'd be doing something, and I wouldn't die under a cloud of flies. Images of my three girls came to mind, and I reckoned they might someday know that their dad died trying.

This was my last chance.

## Night March

All afternoon lying under my ragtag shelter in the dirt of the dry riverbed, I tried to rest as well as I could, conserving my last measure of energy. But because of the sun's swing across the sky, I had to constantly shuffle to stay within the sliver of shade afforded by the shelter. The swarms of insects that zeroed in on my eyes, ears, mouth, and nose offered no relief.

By 5:00 p.m. the sun was about to drop behind the ridge to the west, and as it was only an hour or two from dusk, the temperature began to cool slightly. I was eager to get moving.

I removed a few essentials from my pack and placed them in a small bag to carry by hand: a piece of string, a razor blade, a few matches, my map, my empty water bottle, and my compasses.

I pulled my filthy socks back onto my pitiful feet and slipped on my tattered shoes, hoping they would last. Then I asked God once more for his blessing, guidance, and wisdom: *Lord, I hope this is what you want me to do. You gave me these feet. You gave me these legs and this body. Use me, Lord. Guide me.*

Then I was off.

At first I felt good about doing something other than just lying in the dirt and rotting. The level road in the riverbed was a relatively easy walk, but still I moved slowly. I constantly looked to my left and up at the steep mountain I needed to climb. Once the road turned away from the riverbed, the climb became more difficult. I took it step by step. I was able to move in only fifty- to a hundred-foot stretches before I'd have to stop to rest. I would bend over, hands on knees, struggling to catch my breath, forcing myself to exhale slower, mustering more strength for the next push. I didn't dare sit or lie down.

After about an hour and a half, I reached a point where the road, having switched back to the mountainside, now put me at a point where I could look down at the cement camp below. Even though I had walked about two miles up the hill, because of the winding road, I had traveled only about a third of a mile as the crow flies from where I had started.

There was no sign of the hoped-for village over the hill. Still, I was committed and determined to press on for as long as I could. Stomach cramps again racked my body. As I stood there, bent over and trying to catch my breath, I looked back into the dry river valley below. Just beyond the cement camp, perhaps a third of a mile farther downriver, I could just make out a dark area in the valley. It looked familiar. I was puzzled. Soon I realized what it was. I was looking at a grove of cane and bamboo in the riverbed. Was there water down there?

The last time I had looked down into a valley and had seen such a sight, the Lord had led me to water. *Should I go back down the road to the valley below or keep pressing on along this road? God, what should I do? What do you want me to do?*

I really didn't want to go back down that road; I had worked too hard to get this far. I felt that if I went down the hill and found no water, I would never make it back up again. And besides, I was confident that rescue was just over the next hill. *If I go back down and don't find water, I'll be right back where I started a couple of hours ago and even worse off. I'll be more fatigued and more dehydrated.* I stood there for several indecisive minutes and prayed, *Lord, tell me what to do.*

I really wanted to press on, but something tugged at my subconscious. Once before, the Lord had revealed to me a green grove, and when I dutifully followed his signs, I was saved by the miracle of the spring of sweet water. Now here I was, essentially arguing with God. He appeared to be revealing another enticing green grove below, and I knew then what I must do.

I turned and began my descent back down the hill.

Going downhill didn't take nearly as long as going up. Soon I was back at the cement camp, and I immediately headed downstream toward the green grove where again I faced a tangled mass of dry thorny vines and land-mine cacti, which by this point I ignored. Before long I was at the edge of the thick grove of the same kind of dry cane I had found on day two. The soil here, though, was different—much softer, like ash. And the grove was drier. The stalks became so thick I had to crawl along the ground of the tangled thatch grove in my search for some sign of water. Choking on the dust, I fought my way into the center of the thick mass. Amid the ash and fine dust, I couldn't find any sign of recent water or growth. Instead, I saw evidence of a past fire. Large swaths of the grove were charred.

Exhausted, I withdrew, and once I was out of the maze, I rolled onto my back gasping and wheezing, unable even to cough or spit up the dust I had inhaled. I implored God: *Lord, why did you lead me here? What did you want me to find? What is it you want me to do? Please tell me. Show me!* I was so tired and beyond frustrated, but I tried not to get angry. *Whatever you want, Lord... Whatever you want.*

## Another Night in the Desert

In the darkness with the light of a beautiful half moon, I stared at the mountain I had descended just hours before. I looked heavenward and pleaded, *Why, Lord? Why did you show me this grove? Why did you lead me off the mountain?* I was overwhelmed, discouraged, and too disheartened to wait for an answer. With a bit more energy, I would have been furious. I felt like David when he wrote, "I cry aloud to the Lord; I lift up my voice to the Lord for mercy. I pour out before him my complaint; before him I tell my trouble."[7]

I staggered back to the cement camp and collapsed facedown in the dirt. After some time I sat up and returned to my conversation with God. *Lord, I'm so very sorry for all the bad decisions that put me in this situation. It is all my fault, and I know that only you can help me. Please, Lord, I know you had a reason for bringing me that sweet water two days ago. I know, Lord, that it was you who placed that dirt road before me this morning. And, Lord, I pray, knowing that you had good reasons for compelling me to turn back and return to this forsaken place. Please, God, make your plan clear to me. If it is your will, please deliver me. But, Lord Jesus, whatever your will is, I accept it.*

I didn't bother setting up my shelter again. I saw no reason to. At that point I doubted I would see another dawn, let alone need shelter from the sun. That's how bad I judged my condition to be.

My looming fate saddened me. Anger and fear had come and gone days ago. Now I felt only sorrow. I was filled with so much regret. I was struck by how easy it had been to land myself in my current situation, at how fragile our lives are. To think that less than a week ago I was with my wife in the Lima airport, and my greatest challenge then was how to fill my remaining time in Peru. Now I would almost surely die here, alone in a remote corner of the world. *Oh well,* I thought, *it's not a bad place to die. At least I picked it, and I'm not dying because some distracted driver killed me with a car.*

I sat there for a long time, thinking about these things, weighing my situation. In the exhausted and dehydrated fog of my mind, I managed to narrow it all down to two last options. After fifty-three years my entire life had come down to only two choices: die here or make another attempt to climb up the road. That was it.

Each day of our lives is filled with hundreds of choices: what to do, what to wear, what to eat, what to do first or second or last, and so on. We are consumed by countless decisions. A simple trip to the mall forces us to make multiple decisions—where to park, what to purchase or not, where to eat, whether or not we should catch a movie. We take this plethora of options we face daily for granted. Then there are the big decisions: career choice, marriage, family, finances, education, and vacation planning, just to name a few. Decisions are part of life in the time and society we live in.

But there I was with no such burden of an abundance of choice. I was a free man. I had it easy. My entire universe came down to only two choices, and I had just one decision to make: option A, sit there and die, or option B, try to walk out.

Neither choice was very appealing.

I was thankful that at least I had a choice. Some people don't have that luxury. I figured that God gave me the legs, lungs, heart, and body that were still more or less functional, and I should use them.

Then I thought back to Glenn as he had appeared to me in the canyon on my second night. He had asked, "Hey, Scott. You comin'?"

Yes!

With that thought in mind, I chose to walk out or die trying.

# Day 5

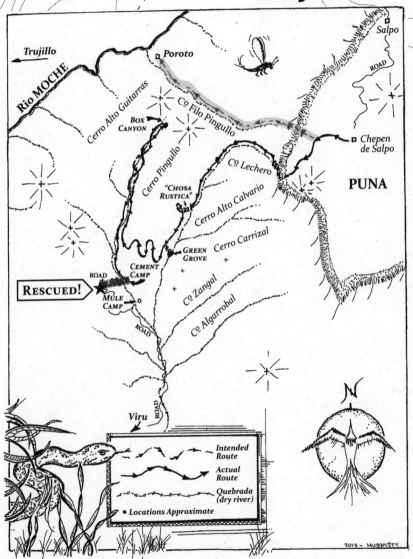

Trujillo

Rio MOCHE

Poroto

Salpo

ROAD

Cerro Alto Guitarras

BOX CANYON

Cº Filo Pingullo

Chepen de Salpo

Cerro Pingullo

Cº Lechero

PUNA

"CHOSA RUSTICA"

Cerro Alto Calvario

GREEN GROVE

Cerro Carrizal

CEMENT CAMP

ROAD

RESCUED!

MULE CAMP

Cº Zangal

Cº Algarrobal

ROAD

Viru

ROAD

Intended Route

Actual Route

Quebrada (dry river)

• Locations Approximate

N

2013 – HUBBARTT

# 14

# Dance of Death

The fact is, I think I am a verb instead of a personal pronoun. A verb is anything that signifies to be; to do; or to suffer. I signify all three.

—Ulysses S. Grant

Sometimes you just gotta press on.

—Glenn D. Hubbartt Jr.

*Monday, 7 November 2011, 0130 Hours, Sud Quebrada El Peñón (8° 10'10.88 S, 78° 48'01.34" W—Elevation 2,253')*

The rattle of the plastic sheet as it whipped away from my exposed legs was followed by the night's biting chill. It was a really rude wake-up call in the middle of yet another dark and frigid night in the high Andean desert.

Clumsily, I rolled over, shifted positions, and struck my elbow on a stone as I shuffled to get up to my knees. Then, panting from the effort, I knelt in the cold and struggled to urinate but was only able to deposit a few drops onto a scrap of plastic cupped in my hand. This I quickly lifted to my lips and choked down. I knew the disgusting exercise was doing more harm than good, but I was too thirsty to let the liquid go to waste.

I then dropped heavily onto the sharp rocks, feeling little pain. I was beyond that. As I lay beneath a beautiful canvas of stars set against the blackest of nights, a singular, dreadful thought enveloped me like an ominous, heavy dark cloak: *Today I will die, so this is how it ends.*

It was early Monday morning, November 7, my fifth day lost. My cracked watch said it was 1:30 a.m., too early to start walking. Dawn was still a few hours away. I needed to get some sleep and harness what little strength I could muster before my last attempt to get out of the canyon and, if possible, survive.

I needed one more miracle.

## Preparing for the Inevitable

I usually welcome new experiences and adventures. Life, I have found, is a collection of so many new and wonderfully exciting events. Death would certainly be a new one. Not too exciting and certainly not wonderful, but it, too, would be a totally new experience. In my delirium I thought, *Unlike most of life's lessons, there will be nothing for me to learn from this one. No one will ever know what happened to me. My legacy—all I will leave behind—will be questions, sadness, and so much pain inflicted on the undeserving people back home who love and care about me.*

I knew that, short of a huge miracle, the slowly approaching dawn would be my last. I wasn't so much afraid as I was sad and filled with regret. I had come to accept what increasingly looked like the inevitable—my impending death. *This will be my last day on earth,* I kept thinking. As I lay there, I couldn't escape the troubling irony that exactly four years ago was Glenn's last full day alive. He had died on November 8, 2007, and now it looked as if my turn had come.

*Oh well…this isn't a bad place to die.*

I had come to believe that the desert was a clean and pure place. The ordeal I had been through over the past five days had whittled me down to my basic and essential elements. Although I must have looked terrible—beat up, filthy, and dried out—I felt purged and cleansed. In the desert there was little room for clutter, secrets, or shame.

I knew I had miserably messed up and was a victim of my own undoing. Pride, arrogance, and overconfidence were leading to my demise.

Fairness was not a factor; my time had come. I knew *how* I would die. I knew *where* I would die. And I knew *why* I would die. But most disturbing was the realization that there was almost nothing I could do about it—*almost*.

I also knew that my bodily reserves were spent and death was way overdue. Still, I retained a speck of hope. I knew I had to make one final effort, one last push to save myself.

*Dying will be easy,* I thought, *but the task ahead will be hard.* I mentally prepared myself, then turned to the Lord one last time. Whispering through cracked lips I prayed, "Lord Jesus, I accept your will. If this is what you want, God, please be with me. Give me strength and wisdom."

Then, with the ever-present shadow of death hovering over me, yet with resolve in my heart, I once again surrendered to exhaustion and drifted off to a last couple of hours of precious rest.

## Facing the Final Dawn

As the darkness lifted, I gathered my small bag and my empty, battered water bottle and set off once more.

I dreaded the thought of climbing the hill again, but I did so, one small step after another, shuffling upward. I didn't bother to look at my watch. Time meant little to me at that point. My hips bothered me considerably, probably from lying on the rough gravel and stones the past four nights. More than once during those nights I had awakened to a stabbing pain in my core and was forced to shift positions frequently. There seemed to be no way to lie where I could find relief. That, combined with being severely dehydrated and traipsing through this rugged landscape, had done my joints no good. Thankfully, the countless cuts and scrapes that covered every inch of my exposed skin no longer stung or burned. My focus was on other, more pressing concerns.

I still had a singular, urgent need—*water.* Thirst consumed most of my conscious thoughts. I was parched. I craved water. My throat was raw, and at night more than once I had forced my tongue from the roof of my mouth with my fingers, fearing that the drying, sticky tissue might strangle me as I slept.

The climb up the first hill went very slowly. In the faint light of dawn, I could barely make out tire tracks and footprints that had been invisible to me the night before. After what seemed an eternity but must have been only an hour or two, I reached the point where the night before I had stopped and turned back. Panting, I briefly surveyed the cement camp below me, then turned and staggered on. As I crested the first ridge and descended into the next vale, I saw that I faced another steep climb over the next ridge. I tried to sing praise songs but could not remember many of the words. With my head spinning all I could croak out repeatedly was, "Thank you, Jesus... Thank you, Jesus... Thank you, Lord, for saving me."

After I climbed still another hill, I came to a split in the dirt track. Oh no! I hadn't expected there to be other roads. As I looked up one and then the other, I was befuddled. My mind was clouded, and I struggled to make a decision. I glanced at my feet and noticed there seemed to be more vehicle tracks and footprints on the road to my right. So I decided to go with the crowd.

After another third of a mile or so, I came to another junction and used the same criterion to make the decision.

The dirt road dipped and wound its way along the hillside, which was virtually void of any plants except for a few clusters of dead grass and the occasional dried-up cactus. With my head down, I plodded along step by step. I had little awareness of anything, even my own body. All I seemed to be aware of were my eyes, and the struggle to keep them focused on the faint footprints in the rough road, and my feet, which I carefully and methodically plopped one after the other as best I could to slowly propel myself forward. I felt numb all over and could hardly feel the heat on my back, but I knew from the waves coming up off the dirt road that at 8:30 a.m. it was already very hot.

Slowly, step by step, I trod, my scraping feet occasionally catching on a ripple in the track, causing me to stumble. The sky was clear, but there was no wind or any sound. I might as well have been hiking on the moon. I felt like a walking dead man, which wasn't far from the truth.

## Whole for Heaven

During the First Gulf War, I had spent six excruciating months in the Arabian Desert. Most of the time was extremely boring, with the exciting days maybe totaling six weeks. Fortunately, it all turned out okay—for the good guys at least.

Near the end of the conflict, Saddam Hussein's massive army was in tatters and surrendering in droves to coalition forces. Many of the poor fellows simply followed the instructions on the leaflets dropped across the lines, instructing the Iraqi soldiers to put down their arms and walk south. They did so in the thousands. Once they reached our forces, they were captured and received clean water, hot meals, and medical treatment. Some with the worst injuries were brought for advanced treatment to the air base where I was stationed.

One day I helped unload from a transport plane an old guy whose leg had been blown off. He was clutching to his chest his severed and badly decayed limb, carefully wrapped in clear plastic. An interpreter told me that the soldier held on to his severed leg because he feared dying and being turned away from heaven because he was not whole. The translator then lit a cigarette, more to stifle the stench than to smoke, and told me this guy was like the walking dead. He said the soldier had walked for three days through the desert before he stepped on one of his own land mines. When coalition forces found him, he was near death yet refused to be air-evacuated without his leg. An allied soldier picked up the mangled, rotting limb, wrapped it in plastic, and gave it to the soldier so he could go to heaven as a whole person.

In the Andes in my delirium, I thought about that Iraqi soldier clutching his severed leg. What was he walking to before he stepped on that mine? Did he even know? Certainly I knew what awaited me if I could somehow get out of this desert. I had family and friends and a very good life to look forward to. He, on the other hand, had walked toward a great void. It was amazing to think that he was walking toward his enemy—toward defeat, toward the great unknown. *And it's strange,* I thought, *that someone would have such faith in a God that would turn him away if he were not physically whole.*

- - - - -

As I slowly climbed the mountain, bizarre and confusing thoughts rushed through my pounding head. Struggling up that hill, I startled myself by crying out, "Where is everybody?" And then, just as quickly, I responded, "Why'd I say that?" *Great! Now I'm having a conversation with myself!*

Then, as if I were a poet, I said out loud, "I follow the tracks of men I can only dream of, to places I'll never go." Then I thought, *What a strange thing to say.* I don't know why I said that or why I remember it so clearly.

The next few hours are a blur. As I walked, I looked down at the tracks beneath me in the roadbed. At times I felt as if I were on a moving walkway going the wrong direction. At other times I felt as though I were standing still, going nowhere, the same strip of dirt passing below my feet again and again.

By now it was past noon, and I was hot and weary beyond words. I wanted to stop and rest. I wanted to sleep, but I didn't dare. *If I lie down now,* I thought, *I may never get up.* I had to stay on my feet. I had to keep going. When the road took a dip, I thanked the Lord for the easy road. When I began to climb again, I thanked him for the dip to come after the next hill.

At one point a song from my past came like a cool wind to my mind. I began to croak, "As the deer pants for the water, so my soul longs after You." I smiled at the memory of the song, which echoes Psalm 42:1. It was from a time more than ten years earlier when I was stationed in Holland, assigned to a Dutch air force base that had no chapel or chaplain. However, we did have a local American missionary couple, Darryl and Cheryl DeVries, who held weekly services on base for the American service members and their families. Whenever the call for a song request came during our Sunday meetings, I would inevitably pick "the deer song." My daughters gave me a hard time because I always picked the same song. I didn't care, because I really liked it.

I had not heard or sung that beautiful hymn in nearly a decade, but as I struggled along, I sang that line over and over again with a smile cracking my dry lips: "As the deer pants for the water, so my soul longs after You."

I stopped frequently—bent over, hands on knees, elbows locked—struggling to catch my breath. I'd then debate one more time the merits of taking a short five-minute nap, only to talk myself out of the temptation. Then I would press on.

After one such rest stop, I found I could no longer remember any of the words to the deer song. My mind was mush. It was a new low.

15

# Found

I once was lost but now am found.

—John Newton, "Amazing Grace"

*Monday, 7 November 2011, 1330 Hours, On a Dirt Road*
*High in the Mountains West of Quebrada El Peñón and North*
*of Río Las Salinas*
*(8º 10'49.79" S, 78º 48'21.18" W—Elevation 2,253')*

Once again I stopped and bent over, panting. As I raised my head, I saw something strange, something different. Far, far ahead on the road were tiny yellow and orange bouncing balls. At first I thought that the words to a song would appear beneath them, but then I realized the colored shapes were following the contour of the road. Was this some kind of weird optical illusion, a mirage?

I stood transfixed. *Are they birds? Pheasants perhaps?* Immediately I realized how ridiculous that was. I closed my eyes and imagined I was looking at colored pinheads on a map. Looking once more down the road, I cocked my head, squinted my eyes, and tried to figure them out. *What…are…they?*

Just then, tiny, blurry stick figures formed below each ball. They were not still. They were moving slowly and wove back and forth among themselves. Two yellow dots led the cluster, and a single orange dot lingered behind the group.

*Men! They are men!* "The cement workers," I cried out. I jumped and yelled, waving my arms. "Boy, are you late for work!" I screamed hoarsely. They did not respond and continued their slow progress up the road. I experienced a moment of terror that I was imagining it all. Suddenly I saw one blurry figure point in my direction and wave back at me.

I fell to my knees and wept dry tears, repeating, "Thank you, Lord. Thank you, Lord," over and over.

These men—I counted eight of them, all in hard hats and workmen's clothes—approached me cautiously and with puzzled looks. I heard them speaking in low voices. I was still on my knees, weeping uncontrollably. They didn't know what to think. They had come across a babbling, filthy, beat-up gringo in the middle of nowhere.

*"¡Ayúdame! ¡Ayúdame!"* ("Help! Help!") I cried.

They gathered around me.

*"¿De dónde habrá venido?"* ("Where did he come from?")

*"¿Estará borracho?"* ("Is he drunk?")

Then, seeing several of them carrying water bottles, I begged for some, gesturing. *"¿Tiene agua? Necesito agua, señor...por favor"* ("Do you have water? I need water, sir...please"), I croaked.

One stocky man, whose name I later learned was Ruben, quickly handed over his bottle. It was obviously not spring water and likely from a questionable source, but I tipped it up and drank deeply of the sweet, cloudy fluid. I simply could not believe it. This was too good to be true.

Then speaking directly to me, one of them asked, *"¿De dónde vienes?"* ("Where are you coming from?")

*"La puna,"* I replied.

*"¿La puna?"* he said suspiciously. *"¿Dónde está su camión?"* ("Where is your truck?")

*"No tengo camión. Caminé. Estoy perdido."* ("I don't have a truck. I walked. I'm lost.")

*"Imposible!"* was their collective response. *"¡Está muy lejos!"* ("It's very far!")

"Yes. I've been lost for five days. No food. No water," I explained in my best, rough Spanish.

Between sobs and drinks from the water bottle, I briefly told them how I was going to Poroto but got lost. *"¿Cerca de Poroto?"* ("Are we close to Poroto?") I asked. They didn't know.

There were some more quick murmurs and whispered discussions. Finally one of the younger men urged the others to leave me and keep going. He said something about it getting late. A few of them began to walk away, but Ruben and two others stayed behind with me for a few moments. They offered me some food, some sort of meat wrapped in bread and foil. I turned it down, thinking my stomach could not handle it. Then a small tangerine appeared from a pocket and was offered to me, along with a full bottle of cloudy water. I took both gratefully, thanking them and Jesus openly.

*"Sí,"* Ruben said to me, pointing upward. *"¡Un milagro! ¡Gracias a Dios!"* ("It's a miracle! Thanks to God!")

Ruben indicated they had to go but that *el jefe* (the boss) would be coming along in a truck soon. He told me to stay put and assured me I would be okay. As he started to turn and walk away, I thanked him for rescuing me. Ruben suddenly turned back to me and said, *"No, señor. Dios lo rescató a usted."* ("No, sir. God rescued you.")

I sat on the side of the road and savored the deliciously warm bottle of water. I was so very grateful, giving nonstop prayers of thanksgiving for my deliverance. I then brought the tangerine up to my nose, and it smelled so good that I sobbed. It occurred to me that throughout this whole ordeal I could not recall having smelled anything. There was no recollection whatsoever of scents or smells. But here in my hand was the sweetest and most fragrant thing I could imagine.

The pungent aroma of the tangerine caused my stomach to knot and my desiccated saliva glands to ache in anticipation. I slowly peeled the perfect fruit and savored the splendid scent of its flesh and juice. Then, unable to wait any longer, I devoured it, taking long minutes afterward to lick the sticky juice from my filthy hands and wrists. It was simply the best thing I had ever eaten.

About forty-five minutes later I saw a white pickup truck slowly coming up the road. As it approached, I waved frantically. The driver was a thin young man accompanied by an older, heavier guy. When they stopped, I again went over my story in halting Spanish. The thinner man explained he was the boss of the crew that had found me. The guy riding shotgun was named Junior.

At first Junior didn't believe a word of what I said, but the boss did. That's all that mattered! He explained that his men were working on a government contract to build concrete foundations for high-tension electrical power transmission towers being erected in the area. I described the cement camp in the dry riverbed and asked if his men were heading there today. "No," he answered. That cement was positioned for work they would be doing later on—perhaps in a few weeks.

He invited me into the cab of his truck. After stiffly climbing in, I asked how far it was to Poroto. The boss said, *"Poroto! No estás nada cerca de Poroto! Quizás, quieres decir Virú?"* ("Poroto! You're nowhere near Poroto! Maybe you mean Virú?")

"I've never heard of Virú," I said, then brought out my map and asked him to show me where we were. He carefully studied my map, consulted Junior, and after some time unfolded it, searching farther south, far away from my intended destination of Poroto. After a bit he pointed to a green-shaded area along the coast far south of Trujillo and then traced his finger inland and slightly northward.

*"¡Acá! ¡Acá! Está Virú!"* ("There. That's Virú!") the crew boss announced. Next he slowly ran his finger diagonally up the map, studied it some more, and circled a three-inch area saying, *"Más o menos estamos por aquí."* ("We are somewhere around here.") With that he put the truck in gear and started down the bumpy road.

I was dumbfounded. He had pointed to an area far to the south and west of where I believed I was. *How could that be?* I asked myself as we bounced down the road. How could I have been so far off? Right then, however, I was more concerned with getting out of these mountains and back to civilization.

The boss offered to take me into Virú, but he would not be able to do so until the end of the day. In the meantime, he explained, I would be taken to his camp to rest. The ride to the camp took about forty-five minutes. Along the way I noticed numerous side roads jutting off to the left and right of the primary road, which itself twisted and turned through the hills and across a couple of dry streambeds.

The boss told me that he was from Colombia and was very happy to have this contract. It was hard work, but he had a good crew, and their work was on schedule. I then asked him his name, to which he replied, smiling, "¿*Mi nombre? ¡Mi nombre es* Harrison, *como* Harrison Ford*!"* ("My name? My name is Harrison, like Harrison Ford!") He explained that his parents had seen the movie *Raiders of the Lost Ark* in the 1980s and loved it so much that they'd named him after the leading man.

## The Mule Camp

We pulled into a small quebrada containing a rustic work camp. A tent was pitched not far from a large tarp suspended on rough poles. The camp, which included a crude corral with a large plastic water tank next to it, looked like a movie set for a Western.

Twelve burros were tethered in a line together, all loaded with bags of cement similar to those I'd seen at the cement camp. As we pulled in, men were moving the string of animals out of the area and up a steep trail along the valley wall. Harrison spat off some instructions to a young man under the tarp, and then he showed me to a place next to the tent where I could rest in the shade. He said that I could eat if I wanted to and that there was plenty of water.

I thanked him profusely, shaking his hand in both of mine. Harrison told me he'd be back later to get me and then climbed back into his pickup and drove off. As the truck pulled away, I saw Junior looking over his shoulder at me, laughing and shaking his head.

I was left alone at the camp with a man I took to be both the cook and the camp master. He was naturally curious about the odd character—a filthy, emaciated foreigner deposited into his care. I did my best to explain my story, and he shook his head in disbelief.

At first I sat there in the shade on a dirty but comfortable mattress as the cook worked in the makeshift kitchen, cutting up limp vegetables and gray meat. The conditions were crude, and flies swarmed all around, but I didn't mind. It felt so good to be back among the living. I sipped more water and dozed off.

After a while a line of braying mules woke me. Several men led the pack animals lumbering into camp, trailing more flies and kicking up choking clouds of dust. The mules were untethered, watered, and fed. The muleteers then came over to the shelter as the cook shoveled generous helpings of a stew onto chipped plates. As the men gathered around the rough table, they looked at me with curiosity and suspicion. I'm sure I was a strange sight. The cook offered a brief explanation to the men, which generated a chorus of comments and questions. After their meal they filed back to the corral and reloaded the loudly complaining mules, which were retethered and assembled for a return trip up the mountain.

I rummaged through my little bag and inventoried my few possessions. Among them were a razor blade, a broken pencil with a yard or two of dirty duct tape rolled onto it, and a small coil of thin nylon cord. I offered these meager treasures to the cook, but he looked at me as if I were crazy and set them unceremoniously on a nearby bench.

I reflected on what had happened. Along that long difficult road, I had encountered several splits where the dirt roads headed off in different directions. I was able to stay on the primary track only by following the footprints in the soft dust along the roadbed. It was good I had waited until daylight to walk. If I had taken this road in the darkness, I would not have seen those tracks. And at night I surely would not have lasted long enough to meet up with the workmen I encountered today. It had been critically important that I wait until the morning.

I know now that God worked to draw me in the direction he needed me to go. When I decided to walk out of the cement camp on the fourth night, I didn't get very far. God knew that only the hope of more water in a green grove would soften my stiff neck and compel me to turn back and descend to the cement camp. God needed me to spot that green grove and go back to the riverbed. I was intent on walking out of the canyon that fourth night, but he knew such an attempt would fail. God's plan and timing are always perfect.

— — — — —

I drifted off to sleep and woke up with a start when the cook offered me a plate of steaming meat, rice, and vegetables. Although it looked delicious, I knew I was not ready for solid food. I thanked him and asked instead for more water. He gestured for me to follow him. About fifty yards away there was a large covered plastic water tank with a spigot on the side. He showed me where I could fill my bottle. The water smelled strongly of chlorine but was very welcome all the same.

The cook then motioned for me to go with him farther along the trail, which hugged a small dry creek, where a long hose led to a crude three-sided shelter: a field shower. He said I was welcome to clean up. In fact, he insisted. I was a mess, and even in his foul kitchen, I stood out.

I thanked him and slowly stripped and then stepped into the shower. The hose delivered a dribble of cool, clear chlorinated water above my head, and I savored it as the tiny rivulets spread over my battered body. I ran my rough hands over my arms and shoulders and rejoiced in the sensation. *How could anyone ever take water for granted?* Looking down on the flat rock that formed the shower floor, I was appalled to see the excess water running off and into the dry creek bed. *What an absolute waste!* I clamped the hose shut and just stood there, enjoying the sensation of the moisture on my skin. Reaching for my clothing, I could not believe its condition. *Was I really wearing these filthy things?* I had no choice but to put back on the frayed and dusty rags. Once dressed, I returned to the makeshift field kitchen.

There I found six men crowded around the little table, happily chattering and enjoying their afternoon meal. As I walked up, they became silent. I greeted them and sat down on the nearby dirty mattress. One of them, obviously the most boisterous of the bunch, said to me, *"¡Ah, así es que tú eres el gringo perdido!"* ("So, you're the lost gringo, eh!")

*"Sí."*

*"Bueno, haber cuéntanos tu historia. ¿De dónde vienes? ¿Qué pasó?"* ("So tell us your story. Where did you come from? What happened?")

In my broken Spanish I once again went through my story as they listened intently. Occasionally one of them would make comments or ask a question. One of the more quiet men said to me, *"Dios lo estaba protegiendo, señor. Usted fué muy afortunado."* ("God was looking out for you, mister. You were very fortunate.") Then the boisterous one added, laughing, *"¡Y muy baboso!"* ("And pretty stupid!") I agreed on both counts.

I pulled out my map and asked if they knew where we were. Several of them hovered over the chart and entered into intense deliberation that bordered on a heated argument. They could not agree as to exactly where on the map we were. The general consensus was that it was roughly the same area Harrison had identified. I then showed them where I had come from—information they treated with suspicion. I explained how nothing made sense in those mountains and about my confusion and difficulty correlating my map and compass.

*"¡Ah! ¡Brújulas no funcionan aquí!"* ("Hah! Compasses don't work here!") one of the older men said. He went on to explain there were metals in the mountains that made compasses very unreliable. Gesturing to the hills, he went on, *"Algunos dicen que hay demonios en estas montañas dispuestos a confundir y enloquecer a los hombres, pero nosotros sabemos que la causa es por el metal en la tierra!"* ("Some say there are demons in these

mountains intent on confusing men and making them crazy, but we know that it's the metal in the soil!")

"*Sí, sí,*" several of the others agreed.

*Of course! Why had this not occurred to me?* That would explain my erratic compass readings and much of my confusion. How could I have overlooked that possibility? I felt ridiculous. Then the boisterous one said, "*¡Sí, hay muchos diablos en las colinas, muchacho!*" ("Yes, there are demons in those hills, young man!") "*¡Pero tu brújula solo te enseña el hierro!*" ("But your compass only sees the iron!")

# 16

# Home

I let it go. It's like swimming against the current. It exhausts you. After a while, whoever you are, you just have to let go, and the river brings you home.

—Joanne Harris, *Five Quarters of the Orange*

A man travels the world over in search of what he needs and returns home to find it.

—George Augustus Moore, *The Brook Kerith*

Home is the nicest word there is.

—Laura Ingalls Wilder

*Monday, 7 November 2011, 1500 Hours, The Mule Camp,*
*Near Río Las Salinas*
*(8º 11'21.56" S, 78º 47'29.63" W—Elevation 1,952')*

I spent the remainder of the afternoon resting near the kitchen while the cook ignored me. Now and then workmen drifted in and out, and each time the cook migrated out of my earshot and in a low voice—accompanied with a lot of head shaking—talked about this stranger in their camp. Strings of mules came, were watered, then reloaded, and went out again.

Late in the afternoon first one then another train of mules came into camp and were untethered, fed, and let loose into the corral. When the crude wooden racks strapped to their backs were removed, I saw horrible open red sores on a few of the beasts. The cook passed a jug of gasoline he used to start his fire to one of the muleteers, who roughly grabbed the ear of the beast and tossed a towel over the animal's eyes. Then he splashed the gasoline onto the poor creature's back. The animal bucked violently and wailed pitifully. After a few cruel slaps to its snout, the beast settled down and was led to join the others.

I became anxious at these signs of the end of the workday in the camp. Would Harrison return for me? Before long a beat-up school bus pulled up, carrying several workmen. The muleteers climbed aboard, and it left. I asked the cook about my ride into Virú, and he said that Harrison would be coming soon. The sun was fast descending behind the hills, and with it the desert air began to cool rapidly. Shortly thereafter a few pickup trucks came along the road and stopped. The cook gestured for me to walk out to the road and join the men gathering alongside it. I limped over to the men, and they greeted me warmly. Seeing that I was cold, one of them lent me his jacket while we waited.

Just as the light was fading, Harrison appeared in his white truck, followed by an old bus. The men wished me well, and most piled onto the bus. Harrison told me and four of the men to get into his vehicle, and almost instantly we were bouncing along the dry riverbed and heading south. I was ecstatic. Finally I was on my way out of these mountains.

## The Way Back

It took us about an hour and a half to get into Virú, and by then it was dark. After dropping the men off at different corners in the town, Harrison and Junior drove me through the city to a shop that served as a bus stop.

A beat-up bus sat along the curb, and an overweight young girl stood at the door and announced "Trujillo!" as its destination. I fished out my emergency three hundred dollars from my secret belt and offered it all to my new friends, but they refused. Seeing the large American bills in my hand, Harrison told me to put them away. "It's not safe," he warned me, "to flash around money like that."

Harrison shut off his truck and walked me over to the girl who was selling tickets at the door of the bus. He paid the four-sols fare for me, wished me well with a handshake and a slap on the back, and said, "Here you go, amigo," handing me the bus ticket with a smile. "Your coach." He also handed me a fresh bottle of water along with a few extra sols. "For a taxi in Trujillo," he added.

I was speechless and hugged him tightly, thanking him. Harrison then said to me, "I'm glad you found my men today."

"I had a lot of help," I responded.

I again tried to push my dollars into his hand, but he refused any payment, saying, "Hey, you gave us something new to talk about up there. We'll be talking about you for weeks!"

Laughing, Junior leaned out his window and offered to take my money, but Harrison pushed his smiling face back into the truck.

As we parted, I noted that both Harrison and I had wet eyes.

I boarded the bus to the gawks of the other passengers, who no doubt had never seen a stranger in such a condition. I don't remember the bus pulling away for the hourlong trip to Trujillo because I was already asleep, clutching to my chest the wonderfully cool and clear two-and-a-half-liter bottle of water Harrison had bought me at the bus stop.

In Trujillo, I stepped off the bus at the small, noisy combi station. I felt like an alien. Had it really been less than a hundred hours since I had left this place? In that short time I'd taken a "short" walk to the edge of my life.

So much seemed different. So many people. So much noise. The locals' stares confirmed how awful I must have looked. Despite the rudimentary shower back at the mule camp, I was still covered in filth. My clothes stank, and my skin was covered with scratches, scrapes, and other signs of abuse. To think, just a few days before, I was grossed out with Mr. Whiskers drooling on my shoulder!

But still, I felt *great*! I was back among the living. What a wonderful thing!

I walked painfully out to the street, stood there, and looked around. "Thank you, Lord," I whispered. It was just after 9:00 p.m., and many taxis darted and wove through the streets. Scores of people, heading home from work, dinner, or the market, crowded the sidewalks. Though I had visited the city a dozen times, I'd never realized just how alive and vibrant Trujillo was.

Everywhere people flowed and ebbed. Across the street a boy was calling it a day, gathering up his bathroom scale that he stood vigilantly behind every day, offering to read your weight for a few centavos. Next to him two old men stood intently debating some issue. So much energy! I just soaked it in for a few moments.

I took a few sips of water, as if I still needed to ration it. Then an obscenely loud, honking taxi caught my attention.

I climbed in and directed him toward José and Sheila's house.

- - - - -

The evening was clear and mild when the taxi pulled up in front of the familiar residence. I stepped onto the curb and stood there for a few moments, savoring the sights and sounds of humanity around me. Before going inside, I said another prayer of thanks. Then, still clutching my precious bottle of water, I reached through the grate. Finding the door locked, I rang the bell. After a moment José looked over the second-floor balcony and cried out, "*¡Carajo! Scotty!*" He dropped the key to me.

I slowly and painfully pulled myself up the stairs and waddled into their house. I was greeted by José and Sheila and several of their friends. Sheila was beside herself with relief. Ignoring my horrid condition, she tearfully hugged me tightly, followed by José. Seeing my appearance and the way I walked, Sheila's friend Chela said to another woman, "*¡Yo creo* *que lo han violado!"* ("I think he's been raped!") Hearing her, I croaked back, *"¡Mi dignidad está intacta!"* ("My dignity is intact!"), causing all of them to laugh. I promised to explain everything later. All I wanted to do was take a shower and get into some clean clothes.

The guests were gone by the time I came back downstairs. And I told Sheila and José my story, all of it, from beginning to end. Between small sips of precious water, I related the tale of my attempt to follow Felipe Lám's journey between Poroto to Chepén, of becoming hopelessly lost, and of nearly dying. I explained to them my struggle to survive and to stay spiritually focused.

Finally I told them how God saw me through with grace and his amazing miracles.

## Thankful for Life

After resting the next day, I rose on Wednesday feeling much better. I caught the first available flight back to Lima and then on to Texas. On my second night home, I met my daughter Christina and her husband, Eric, for dinner at a local market. I was so emaciated that at first Eric did not recognize me and walked right past me. Over a simple meal I told them my story.

After two days of being home, resting and regaining strength, I boarded a plane for Georgia, where Carito was on duty. I anxiously looked forward to reuniting with mi vida.

She picked me up at the airport and was shocked at my appearance. Once we were on the highway, I began to tell her my story. As she drove, my bride was captivated, amazed, and astonished with what I told her. She shook her head repeatedly. Once I finished my tale, I answered her questions.

As the miles passed, we fell silent…both thankful I was safe and alive.

And thankful we were together.

I treasure my wife, mi vida, Carito—Carolina.

# 17

# Reflections

It's what you know after you know it all that counts.

—Harry S. Truman

However, I consider my life worth nothing to me; my
only aim is to finish the race and complete the task the
Lord Jesus has given me—the task of testifying to the
good news of God's grace.

—Acts 20:24

As my body gradually recovered from my many aches, pains, and abuses, I began to assess what had happened. Not just what had gone wrong, but more important, why I had survived and what I was to learn and take away from my experience.

With the very first step off the puna, I had started down the wrong path. I was lost from beginning to end. My compasses were useless, and I ended up following a path that ultimately had me forty miles off course and caused me to lose thirty pounds along the way. But despite the numerous minor injuries—cuts, scrapes, bruises, and the beating I put my body through—it was thirst that became my most pressing problem. I needed water to survive and had far too little of it.

Had I known just how geographically off I was before I departed from the high puna into that spectacular but terrifying gorge, I would have turned back then and there. Instead, I felt supremely confident and was sure that later in the day I would be at a village somewhere in the valley, looking for a comfortable bed and a good night's rest. Still, God chose to save me.

I have only God to credit with my salvation—both spiritual and, in this case, physical. Despite my best efforts in doing virtually everything wrong, he spared my life. And it is not just that he spared me but how he chose to do so that makes my story worth telling.

It has been more than two years since my unforgettable journey, and I am still trying to fully appreciate the gift I was given—*more than life itself,* which we too often take for granted. Like the sole survivor of a plane crash, a cancer survivor, or a released hostage, I know I was spared for a reason. My survival was no less than miraculous, and I still struggle to understand the meaning of it all. I was allowed to survive my ordeal and make it out of the Peruvian desert for a reason. My chore now is to understand, appreciate, and share the story of this gift.

## A Priceless Education

Upon my retirement from the air force in 2004, after twenty-eight years of service in uniform, I found myself wondering what to do next with my life. I was still relatively young. I had two grown and independent daughters and another daughter nearly there. I was modestly secure financially and had a loving and supportive wife who has always encouraged me to follow my dreams. Life was good.

About then I entered a hectic period of my life. I enrolled in a graduate program in history and a postgraduate program in Latin American studies. At the same time, for personal satisfaction, I dived into writing an exhaustive book on my family's genealogy. During this same time frame, I was also shuttling between south Texas and Nebraska to assist my ailing parents. And whenever possible I indulged my wanderlust.

So after leaving the air force, between studying, writing, and helping my parents, I traveled frequently and widely. Along the way I fantasized about the other amazing things I had previously only dreamed of, like jumping on trains and riding as a rail tramp across the country or building and sailing a small boat down the Ohio and Mississippi Rivers, much like my ancestor James Hubbartt did.

While visiting Peru, I considered buying a moto trike and riding it back to Texas. I also planned on venturing to Bolivia to look for airplane crash sites and even hoped to visit San Vicente in the Tupiza region, where the legendary Butch Cassidy and the Sundance Kid supposedly met their end. I also gave serious thought to making my way to Villavicencio, Colombia—the last great gathering site of working DC-3 "Gooney Bird" aircraft—where I hoped to fly on one. I looked for ways to travel overland to remote Paraguay, and, of course, there was the dream of retracing Felipe Lám's footsteps into the high puna.

My bucket list had quite a few items, and I hoped to write about all these adventures. In many ways I was like a boy in a candy shop. I later attributed these fantasies to a sort of midlife crisis. After losing my brother, my father, and my mother in a span of just four years, I was probably trying to squeeze a whole lot of living into a small amount of time.

Since my misadventure in the Andes, however, all these dreams have slid off my radar screen. While I still thirst for travel and hope to pursue a few more adventures, my list has diminished dramatically. After my near-death experience, the bottom line for me is this: *God* is in control, and *he* has a plan for us. Regardless of how lost we are—and that lostness can as easily occur in a remote canyon as well as any area of life—we need to acknowledge him, ask him into our lives, and seek his wisdom and knowledge. It is also important to know we have a purpose greater than serving and satisfying our own desires. All of us have opportunities to share the message of God's grace with others.

In the first two days of my ordeal, when things began to go very, very badly and my repeated cries to God for help seemed unheard, I despaired, and my faith was shaken. I wondered where the Lord was. *Why would he allow me to go through this ordeal?* I asked over and over. *After all, it was Jesus who said, "If you believe, you will receive whatever you ask for in prayer"* and *"Ask and it will be given to you; seek and you will find; knock and the door will be opened to you. For everyone who asks receives; the one who seeks finds; and to the one who knocks, the door will be opened."*[8]

As a flawed and broken man, I knew that my stubbornness and self-ish ambitions, not to mention my lack of wisdom, had landed me in a desolate and remote place, perhaps to die. I frequently turned to God for guidance. Before this experience, I don't think I had been listening very well for what he was saying to me. I now know that he wanted me to ask him what his desires were. I needed to find out what he wanted. I needed to put him first; I needed to submit. I needed to approach him on my knees.

When I was lost and spotted the first green grove of vegetation in the canyon below, then climbed down seeking relief from my torment, I used all my skills and training to search for water. I cut cane, dug into the rocky riverbed, and made solar stills—all to no avail. I squeezed moisture in the form of salty silt through my underwear. But despite all my knowledge, experience, and efforts, my situation only got worse. Then something changed. Instead of asking for, *pleading for* what I wanted—to have God rescue me—I submitted to God's will. I asked him to make me his servant. I resigned myself and accepted his plan, even if that included dying in that canyon. Death surely wasn't my first choice, nor was it easy to put my pride and self-sufficiency aside, but I knew that there was only one path left to me—simple trust. That's when things began to change.

I was blessed with a visit from my brother Glenn, who pointed me back into the green grove. There I was rewarded with another miracle—clear, sweet water bubbling up from the ground where before I had found not a drop.

Over the next few days, more miracles followed. I cannot say that I was beyond struggle or doubts. I drifted back and forth between fear and faith. But even in my suffering and despair, I drew closer to God, acknowledged he was in control, and accepted his goodness and will. That didn't mean my situation was immediately resolved; I still had a long way to go before I was out of danger. But I continued to pray, to submit, and to accept his will.

I have no illusions about what brought me out of that desert. I had very little to do with it. It was only by the direct intervention of God that I was spared. As Ruben, one of the men who found me, said when I thanked him for rescuing me, *"¡No, señor. Dios lo rescató a usted!"* ("No, sir. God rescued you!")

One way to summarize my experience is to say that God allowed me to go to class for ninety-eight hours, and in the process I garnered a lifetime of invaluable lessons and a priceless education. I believe everything happens for a reason. God meant for me to make it through this impossible ordeal and to emerge from that barren wilderness alive. I was given another precious opportunity. I was spared. But why?

First, and obviously the most immediately significant fact, is that, because of God's mercy, I have been given more time on earth and am able to continue to enjoy many joys and pleasures—most meaningfully to me is the time with my wife and family.

Another important reason, I believe, is that I am meant to share this story with you and anyone else who will listen. What is your destiny? Does God have your full attention? Is your life counting in ways that matter to him? Or is your relationship with him—like mine in the past—more about what you want to do with the time and resources you've been given than about following his will?

My simple prayer is that you won't get as lost as I was before you are found in the center of God's purposes for you!

– – – – –

As for completing my journey to retrace Felipe Lám's footsteps into the high puna, I really don't see myself attempting that journey again. I had been to Poroto a couple of times before, and now I have visited the high puna hamlet of Chepén, named for a village many miles to the north where Carito's mother, Evelina, was born and grew up. I experienced the treacherous terrain between Poroto and Chepén, which Felipe and his miners traversed, and surely had a taste of the many difficulties they encountered.

There is no reason for me to revisit that place.

– – – –

I am often asked if I really believe my dead brother came in the flesh to visit me, or if perhaps I was hallucinating. I do believe that Glenn actually came and pointed me in the direction I needed to go. After all, I saw him...I heard him...and I *felt* that gravel flying up from his feet as he ran away.

Reflecting on that startling event, I find even his words prophetic. Glenn didn't say, "Go over there." Instead, he said, pointing toward the green grove, "Hey, Scott. You comin'?"

I have no idea how this miracle visit occurred. All I know is that when I needed him most, my brother was there for me.

Reminds me of someone else I know...

Lord, thank you.

# Afterword

*Monday, 18 June 2012, Midafternoon, Section F, Plot 42,*
*Eagle Point National Cemetery, Eagle Point, Oregon*
*(42° 27'46.97" N, 122° 47'08.86" W—Elevation 1,564')*

A stiff but pleasant breeze blew uphill from the Rogue River valley, and the sun shone brightly as we stepped up to the spot we were looking for. This was the first time I'd visited this place, and I was pleased to feel the serenity and peace of the hallowed ground.

Carito was at my side, and as we stood in this national cemetery, we were both silent in prayer and thought.

He had died near here, a place he loved and spoke fondly of. A flat stone memorial, framed in neatly trimmed grass, sat at my feet:

GLENN D. HUBBARTT JR.

E4 US NAVY
E2 US ARMY
E5 US NAVY
VIETNAM
DATE OF BIRTH: 08/24/1954
DATE OF DEATH: 11/08/2007

I was thankful to have this simple marker to visit, to help me remember. I missed Glenn. I'd much rather have been sitting with my brother over a cup of coffee, exchanging stories of good times past. But that was not to be.

More than seven months had passed since his visit to me in that deep Peruvian quebrada, and it occurred to me just how pleased he must have been to know that he was there when his little brother most needed him.

Carito picked up a small, smooth stone and placed it on the granite marker. Next to it I set a US Navy chief petty officer insignia that had belonged to our dad.

About then, the wind softened to a gentle breeze, carrying with it the pleasant and sweet scents of cedar, Siskiyou primrose, and fir.

I understood then why my brother had liked this place so much.

# Notes

1. Chris McNab, *How to Survive Anything, Anywhere: A Handbook of Survival Skills for Every Scenario and Environment* (Camden, ME: McGraw-Hill, 2004), 57.
2. "Whoever remains stiff-necked after many rebukes will suddenly be destroyed—without remedy" (Proverbs 29:1).
3. 1 John 5:14–15.
4. James 1:5–6.
5. Exodus 17:6; see Exodus 17:1–6 and Numbers 20:8.
6. Proverbs 4:5–6.
7. Psalm 142:1–2.
8. Matthew 21:22; Luke 11:9–10.

# Acknowledgments

This has been an amazing and life-changing experience. Without the love, support, and strength of mi vida, Carito—my companion, my friend, and my mentor—I would never know the true depth of beauty, grace, and compassion. She is simply amazing!

I also have to thank my editor, Bruce Nygren, for having the foresight and wisdom to see the potential in this story—and in me. He has done an amazing job.

But I am most grateful to Jesus Christ, my Savior and my Redeemer. Through him all things are possible.